Charlie Mackesy

Abba's Child is not a book—it's a love letter. Brennan's words wrap you in God's love and lullaby you to sleep in the warmth of his grace. After reading this book, I wanted to race into my father's arms and jump into his lap, giggling, "I'm home, Daddy, I'm home."

MICHAEL YACONELLI
Author of *Dangerous Wonder*

The writing of Brennan Manning reaches out, grabs us, and pulls us in. *Abba's Child* is a book that leaps from the tower of theory and plunges deeply into the stuff of life, the stuff that each of us grapples with on a daily basis. Facing our own reality is painful, traumatic, and ultimately redemptive, as Brennan Manning so artfully illustrates.

DEVLIN DONALDSON
The Vista Grande Company

Honest. Genuine. Creative. God hungry. These words surface when I think of the writings of Brennan Manning. Read him for yourself—you'll see what I mean!

MAX LUCADO
New York Times bestselling author

With prophetic zeal, Brennan speaks to our heart's deepest longing and manages to keep the focus on the One who meets it. Hearing, really hearing, this message—that we "belong"—has and will continue to revolutionize lives.

DR. LARRY CRABB
Founder, NewWay Ministries

BRENNAN MANNING

Abba's child

the cry of the heart for intimate belonging

A NavPress resource published in alliance
with Tyndale House Publishers, Inc.

NavPress is the publishing ministry of The Navigators, an international Christian organization and leader in personal spiritual development. NavPress is committed to helping people grow spiritually and enjoy lives of meaning and hope through personal and group resources that are biblically rooted, culturally relevant, and highly practical.

For more information, visit www.NavPress.com.

Abba's Child: The Cry of the Heart for Intimate Belonging

Copyright © 1994, 2002, 2015 by Brennan Manning. All rights reserved.

A NavPress resource published in alliance with Tyndale House Publishers, Inc.

NAVPRESS is a registered trademark of NavPress, The Navigators, Colorado Springs, CO. The NAVPRESS logo is a trademark of NavPress, The Navigators. *TYNDALE* is a registered trademark of Tyndale House Publishers, Inc. Absence of ® in connection with marks of NavPress or other parties does not indicate an absence of those marks.

Designed by Stephen Vosloo

Cover illustration copyright © Charlie Mackesy. All rights reserved.

The author is represented by the literary agency of Alive Literary Agency, 7680 Goddard St., Suite 200, Colorado Springs, CO 80920, www.aliveliterary.com.

Unless otherwise indicated, all Scripture quotations are taken from *The Jerusalem Bible*, copyright © 1966 by Darton, Longman & Todd, Ltd., and Doubleday & Company, Inc. Scripture quotations marked NIV are taken from the Holy Bible, *New International Version,*® *NIV.*® Copyright © 1973, 1978, 1984, 2011 by Biblica, Inc.® Used by permission. All rights reserved worldwide. Scripture quotations marked NASB are taken from the New American Standard Bible,® copyright © 1960, 1962, 1963, 1968, 1971, 1972, 1973, 1975, 1977, 1995 by The Lockman Foundation. Used by permission.

Some of the anecdotal illustrations in this book are true to life and are included with the permission of the persons involved. All other illustrations are composites of real situations, and any resemblance to people living or dead is purely coincidental.

For information about special discounts for bulk purchases, please contact Tyndale House Publishers at csresponse@tyndale.com, or call 1-800-323-9400.

Cataloging-in-Publication Data is available.

ISBN 978-1-63146-395-2

Printed in the United States of America

23 22 21 20 19 18
9   8   7   6   5   4

Contents

Acknowledgments

I BEGAN WRITING *Abba's Child* with one purpose in mind: to recover the passion that fired my desire to enter the seminary and seek ordination to the priesthood. In the process I discovered that all I wanted from the years of silence and study was to fall in love with God.

After a luncheon with John Eames, then publisher at NavPress, and editorial consultant Liz Heaney in Estes Park, Colorado, I was humbled and gratified by the encouragement they offered to finish the book. Later, Kathy Yanni Helmers brought both professional expertise and a like passion for the Lord that left me more satisfied with a finer redaction than any book I've ever published.

Next, my heartfelt thanks to Lillian Robinson, M.D., and Arthur Epstein, M.D., who guided me through darkness to daylight at a very difficult time in my personal life.

—*Brennan Manning*
1994

Foreword

To be nobody-but-yourself—in a world which is doing its best, night and day, to make you everybody else—means to fight the hardest battle which any human being can fight; and never stop fighting.

WHEN I FIRST READ *ABBA'S CHILD*, these words from E. E. Cummings introduced the preface. This quote and the book that followed spoke to me deeply. In *Abba's Child*, Manning calls attention to a battle for identity that's fought nearly every hour of every day of our lives—a war that's almost completely unacknowledged and yet of extreme importance. Who am I? What is my place in the world? As humans, we are always looking for our true identity against the noisy backdrop of our time. Am I defined by my occupation? My preferences? My passions? My true identity cannot be defined for me. Even the most meaningful moments in politics or music are still not enough to anchor me. And yet as I struggle to define myself in this world, my identity can never come from within. My actions, my art, even my beliefs—all of these need to be rooted in soil other than myself.

And so we begin the solitary journey toward discovering our unique identity. Manning employs a chorus of wise voices who reassure me that though this road may be a lonely one, it is not mine to walk alone. Spiritual giants who have passed this way before have left guideposts along the way, reminding me that I cannot be defined by ever-changing seasons around me, nor can I be guided only by the voices within. Rather, my identity must continue to be found in the love of my Creator Himself. I am loved. Deeply loved. And when I let that love define who I am, I am suddenly free to be myself.

In my songs I'm always looking for light. I'm looking for a window or a mirror—something to frame my experience here on the planet in a new way that allows me to see the truth. Why am I always looking for these windows and doors? Because my ears become deaf, my eyes become blind. I desperately need new ways of looking at the world and at myself. I have a friend who is a visual artist. He defines "the artist" not as someone who creates beauty but as someone who looks for it. And to that end I would say a good songwriter does the same thing: hoping for more than just a new chorus, longing to be free from the same old patterns, to be transformed by the renewing of the mind moment by moment, day by day.

There are far too many voices within my head telling me to quit, telling me to abandon, to find an easier way, to ignore the pain, or to choke it down. To find a book with a host of other voices singing back was a joy. When I first read *Abba's Child* a few years back, I had to write a song in response. So I wrote a tune called "Against the Voices," directly inspired by the words of Manning, Henri Nouwen, Thomas Merton, E. E. Cummings, Julian of Norwich, and the host of others whom Brennan Manning employs.

If this is your first time reading this book, I'm honored to introduce you to it. I pray that Brennan Manning and the timeless voices of the other thinkers quoted within this book might offer you hope. May they remind you that you are loved by the Father-Creator Himself. May they sing and speak into your life against the voices that tell you otherwise.

Jon Foreman, lead singer for Switchfoot
JANUARY 2015, CARDIFF-BY-THE-SEA, CALIFORNIA

Preface to the 2015 Edition

Keep practicing until it lives inside you;
then it will seem foolishly easy
to the unpracticed.

— BILL HOLM, "FRIED CHICKEN IN ICELAND"

PARENTS WITH MULTIPLE CHILDREN say they love all their children equally, just differently. That's true, and maybe not true. I believe some parents have favorites—they just do. And I believe the favorites know who they are.

When it comes to the books written by my friend Brennan Manning, it would be tempting to say "I love them all, just differently." But that's not true. I have a favorite—*Abba's Child*. It was the first of his books I read, my introduction to the ragamuffin man, and maybe that's why it means so much to me—you know, "first love" and all that. Then again, my affection for this book may have to do with the fact that after reading all of his books multiple times, and having the privilege of personally working with him on a handful of his final manuscripts, including cowriting his memoir, I believe the words in this book reveal his heart. They are the *summa* of Brennan Manning. I realize that's a bold statement, but there you have it.

Most writers have a central theme, and all their writings are usually some variation on that theme. While some might say Brennan's theme is the grace of God, I would disagree: It is letting yourself be loved by God. In one of our final conversations, I asked, "Brennan, are you letting God love you?" His reply was classic Brennan: "I'm trying." That's why I began this preface with those words from the late Bill Holm—because letting God love him was something Brennan "kept practicing" throughout his years. What may have appeared "foolishly easy" to those who knew him from the distance of books was far from it. He kept practicing until the very end.

You'll read of "the impostor" in these pages, probably the chapter generating the most discussion since *Abba's Child* was published in 1994. Even now, in the autumn of 2014, that chapter is worth the price of admission. The impostor still runs amok today, aided and abetted by the online-Facebook-Twitter-Instagrammy lives we live.

> *The impostor prompts us to attach importance to what has no importance, clothing with a false glitter what is least substantial and turning us away from what is real. The false self causes us to live in a world of delusion. . . . The impostor demands to be noticed. His craving for compliments energizes his futile quest for carnal satisfaction. His bandages are his identity. Appearances are everything.*

See what I mean? Good grief. Please don't hear me saying the Internet is the culprit here. But the Internet does speed things up, presenting lightning-fast challenges to acceptance and approval and suppression and emotional honesty, just to name a few. If the game of pretense and deception used to be at a gallop, we now play at warp speed. Into this rushing stream, Brennan's plea is evergreen: Live by grace and not by performance. In other words—let God love you. And should you see me out and about somewhere and ask me how I'm personally doing with that, I would answer as my friend so often did: I'm trying.

—*John Blase*
SEPTEMBER 15, 2014

Preface to the 2002 Edition

To be nobody-but-yourself—in a world which is doing its best, night and day, to make you everybody else—means to fight the hardest battle which any human being can fight; and never stop fighting.

— E. E. CUMMINGS

SINCE THE PUBLICATION OF *Abba's Child* in 1994, there have been more comments on "The Impostor" than all the other chapters combined. Well, the impostor continues to reappear in new and devilish disguises. The slick, sick, and sinister impersonator of my true self stalks me even in my sleep. His latest stratagem is to capitalize on my "senior moments," blocking any memory of whether I gobbled my anti-depressant and vitamin pills earlier this morning.

Cunning and crafty, this radical poseur of my egocentric desires exploits my temporary amnesia to make me forget that everything I am is grace, that on my own I cannot receive it, for even receiving it is a gift—that is, the grace to grasp grace is grace. Instead of being nonplussed at the extravagance of God's love, in place of heartfelt gratitude for the sheer and unearned abundance of His gifts, a shameless sense of satisfaction about my accomplishments and a secure feeling of spiritual superiority invade my heart. The impostor is baffling, sly, and seductive. He persuades me to forsake my true self, Abba's beloved child, and, as Cummings notes, become "everybody else."

My greatest difficulty these past years has been bringing the impostor into the presence of Jesus. I am still inclined to flagellate the false self, to beat him mercilessly for self-centeredness, to get disheartened, discouraged, and decide that my alleged spiritual life is merely self-deception and fantasy.

Self-flagellation has a personal history with me. When I was twenty-three years old and a novice in the Franciscan Order in Washington, D.C., the order practiced an ancient spiritual discipline on the Friday nights of Lent. A designated cleric stood flat-footed beside the stairwell on the first floor, slowly and loudly reciting Psalm 51 in Latin. *Miserere me, Domine, secundum misericordiam, tuam . . .*

Meanwhile, the rest of us entered our cells on the second floor clutching a noose-shaped instrument of torture measuring twelve inches long; it was coiled telephone wire. Throughout the duration of the psalm, we whipped our backs and buttocks to extinguish the fire of lust. I flailed away with such reckless abandon that I raised blood blisters on my back.

The following day in the showers, a cleric took one look at my bludgeoned body and reported my condition to the novice master, who reprimanded me for my intemperate zeal. Truth to tell, I was trying desperately to make myself pleasing to God.

Not so with Brother Dismas, who lived in the cell adjacent to mine. I listened as he scourged himself so savagely I feared for both his health and his sanity. I risked a peek through his cracked door: With a bemused smile and a cigarette in his left hand, he was whacking the wall—*thwack, thwack, thwack*. My response? I pitied the poor wretch and returned to my cell with an insufferable sense of spiritual superiority.

Flagellation is not healthy for either the body or the soul.

The impostor must be called out of hiding and presented to Jesus, or feelings of hopelessness, confusion, shame, and failure will stalk us from dawn to dusk. Writing *Abba's Child* was a profound spiritual experience for me, and I wish to share one last reflection. Certain truths can be spoken only from the well of exaggeration. In trying to describe the transcendent mystery of Abba's love, I employed a plethora of adjectives such as infinite, outlandish, mind-bending, ineffable, and incomprehensible. Put them all together and they are still inadequate for one simple reason: *Mystery is spoiled by a word.*

Finally, my old and now retired spiritual director, Larry Hein, who wrote this blessing—"May all your expectations be frustrated, may all your plans be thwarted, may all your desires be withered into nothingness, that you may experience the powerlessness and poverty of a child and sing and dance in the love of God, who is Father, Son, and Spirit"—has come up with another one:

Today on planet Earth, may you experience the wonder and beauty of yourself as Abba's Child and temple of the Holy Spirit through Jesus Christ our Lord.

—*Brennan Manning*
2002

A Word Before

ON FEBRUARY 8, 1956, in a little chapel in Loretto, Pennsylvania, I was ambushed by Jesus of Nazareth. The road I've traveled these last thirty-eight years is pockmarked by disastrous victories and magnificent defeats, soul-diminishing successes and life-enhancing failures. Seasons of fidelity and betrayal, periods of consolation and desolation, zeal and apathy, are not unknown to me. And there have been times . . .

> when the felt presence of God was more real to me than the chair I am sitting on;
> when the Word ricocheted like broken-backed lightning in every corner of my soul;
> when a storm of desire carried me to places I had never visited.

And there have been other times . . .

> when I identified with the words of Mae West: "I used to be Snow White—but I drifted";
> when the Word was as stale as old ice cream and as bland as tame sausage;
> when the fire in my belly flickered and died;
> when I mistook dried-up enthusiasm for gray-haired wisdom;
> when I dismissed youthful idealism as mere naïveté;
> when I preferred cheap slivers of glass to the pearl of great price.

If you relate to any of these experiences, you might want to browse through this book and pause to reclaim your core identity as Abba's Child.

—*Brennan Manning*

Come Out of Hiding

IN FLANNERY O'CONNOR's short story *The Turkey*,[1] the antihero and principal protagonist is a little boy named Ruller. He has a poor self-image because nothing he turns his hand to seems to work. At night in bed he overhears his parents analyzing him. "Ruller's an unusual one," his father says. "Why does he always play by himself?" And his mother answers, "How am I to know?"

One day in the woods Ruller spots a wild and wounded turkey and sets off in hot pursuit. "Oh, if only I can catch it," he cries. He will catch it, even if he has to run it out of state. He sees himself triumphantly marching through the front door of his house with the turkey slung over his shoulder and the whole family screaming, "Look at Ruller with that wild turkey! Ruller, where did you get that turkey?"

"Oh, I caught it in the woods. Maybe you would like me to catch you one sometime."

But then the thought flashes across his mind, *God will probably make me chase that damn turkey all afternoon for nothing.* He knows he shouldn't think that way about God—yet that's the way he feels. If that's the way he feels, can he help it? He wonders if he is unusual.

Ruller finally captures the turkey when it rolls over dead from a previous gunshot wound. He hoists it on his shoulders and begins his messianic march back through the center of town. He remembers the things he had thought before he got the bird. They were pretty bad, he guesses. He figures God has stopped him before it's too late. He should be very thankful. "Thank You, God," he says. "Much obliged to You. This turkey must weigh ten pounds. You were mighty generous."

Maybe getting the turkey was a sign, he thinks. Maybe God wants him to be a preacher. He thinks of Bing Crosby and Spencer Tracy as he enters town with the turkey slung over his shoulder. He wants to do something for God, but he doesn't know what. If anybody were playing the accordion on the street today, he would give them his dime. It is the only dime he has, but he would give it to them.

He wishes he would see somebody begging. Suddenly he prays, "Lord, send me a beggar. Send me one before I get home." God has put the turkey here. Surely God will send him a beggar. He knows for a fact God will send him one. Because he is an unusual child, he interests God. "Please, one right now—" And the minute he says it, an old beggar woman heads straight toward him. His heart stomps up and down in his chest. He springs at the woman, shouting, "Here, here," thrusts the dime into her hand, and dashes on without looking back.

Slowly his heart calms, and he begins to feel a new feeling—like being happy and embarrassed at the same time. Maybe, he thinks, he will give all his money to her. He feels as if the ground does not need to be under him any longer.

Ruller notices a group of country boys shuffling behind him. He turns around and asks generously, "Y'all wanna see this turkey?"

They stare at him. "Where did ya get that turkey?"

"I found it in the woods. I chased it dead. See, it's been shot under the wing."

"Lemme see it," one boy says. Ruller hands him the turkey. The turkey's head flies into his face as the country boy slings it up in the air and over his own shoulder and turns. The others turn with him and saunter away.

They are a quarter of a mile away before Ruller moves. Finally they are so far away he can't even see them anymore. Then he creeps toward home. He walks for a bit and then, noticing it is dark, suddenly begins to run. And Flannery O'Connor's exquisite tale ends with these words: "He ran faster and faster, and as he turned up the road to his house, his heart was running as fast as his legs and he was certain that Something Awful was tearing behind him with its arms rigid and its fingers ready to clutch."

In Ruller many of us Christians stand revealed, naked, exposed. Our God, it seems, is One who benevolently gives turkeys and capriciously takes them away. When He gives them, it signals His interest in and pleasure with us. We feel close to God and are spurred to generosity. When He takes them away, it signals His displeasure and rejection. We feel cast off by God. He is fickle, unpredictable, whimsical. He builds us up only to let us down. He remembers our past sins and retaliates by snatching the turkeys of health, wealth, inner peace, progeny, empire, success, and joy.

And so we unwittingly project onto God our own attitudes and feelings toward ourselves. As Blaise Pascal wrote, "God made man in his own image and man returned the compliment." Thus, if we feel hateful toward ourselves, we assume that God feels hateful toward us.

But we cannot assume that He feels about us the way we feel about ourselves—unless we love ourselves compassionately, intensely, and freely. In human form Jesus revealed to us what God is like. He exposed our projections for the idolatry they are and gave us the way to become free of them. It takes a profound conversion to accept that God is relentlessly tender and compassionate toward us just as we are—not in spite of our sins and faults (that would not be total acceptance), but with them. Though God does not condone or sanction evil, He does not withhold His love because there is evil in us.

Because of how we feel about ourselves, it's sometimes difficult to believe this. As numerous Christian authors, wiser and more insightful than I, have said: We cannot accept love from another human being when we do not love ourselves, much less accept that God could possibly love us.

One night a friend asked his handicapped son, "Daniel, when you see Jesus looking at you, what do you see in His eyes?"

After a pause, the boy replied, "His eyes are filled with tears, Dad."

"Why, Dan?"

An even longer pause. "Because He is sad."

"And why is He sad?"

Daniel stared at the floor. When at last he looked up, his eyes glistened with tears. "Because I'm afraid."

The sorrow of God lies in our fear of Him, our fear of life, and our fear of ourselves. He anguishes over our self-absorption and self-sufficiency. Richard Foster wrote, "Today the heart of God is an open wound of love. He aches over our distance and preoccupation. He mourns that we do not draw near to him. He grieves that we have forgotten him. He weeps over our obsession with muchness and manyness. He longs for our presence."[2]

God's sorrow lies in our refusal to approach Him when we have sinned and failed. A "slip" for an alcoholic is a terrifying experience. The obsession of the mind and body with booze returns with the wild fury of a sudden storm in springtime. When the person sobers up, he or she is devastated. When I relapsed, I had two options: yield once again to guilt, fear, and depression—or rush into the arms of my heavenly Father; choose to live as a victim of my disease—or choose to trust in Abba's immutable love.

It is one thing to feel loved by God when our life is together and all our support systems are in place. Then self-acceptance is relatively easy. We may even claim that we are coming to like ourselves. When we are strong, on top, in control, and as the Celts say, "in fine form," a sense of security crystallizes.

But what happens when life falls through the cracks? What happens when we sin and fail, when our dreams shatter, when our investments crash, when we are regarded with suspicion? What happens when we come face-to-face with the human condition?

Ask any who have just gone through a separation or divorce. Are they together now? Is their sense of security intact? Do they have a strong sense of self-worth? Do they still feel like beloved children? Or does God love them only in their "goodness" and not in their poverty and brokenness as well? Nicholas Harnan wrote,

> *This [brokenness] is what needs to be accepted. Unfortunately, this is what we tend to reject. Here the seeds of a corrosive self-hatred take root. This painful vulnerability is the characteristic feature of our humanity that most needs to be embraced in order to restore our human condition to a healed state.*[3]

The fourteenth-century mystic Julian of Norwich said, "Our courteous Lord does not want his servants to despair because they fall often and grievously; for our falling does not hinder him in loving us."[4] Our skepticism and timidity keep us from belief and acceptance; however, we don't hate God, but we hate ourselves. Yet the spiritual life begins with the acceptance of our wounded self.

Seek out a true contemplative—not a person who hears angelic voices and has fiery visions of the cherubim, but the person who encounters God with naked trust. What will that man or woman tell you? Thomas Merton responds, "Surrender your poverty and acknowledge your nothingness to the Lord. Whether you understand it or not, God loves you, is present in you, lives in you, dwells in you, calls you, saves you, and offers you an understanding and compassion which are like nothing you have ever found in a book or heard in a sermon."[5]

God calls us to stop hiding and come openly to Him. God is the father who ran to His prodigal son when he came limping home. God weeps over us when shame and self-hatred immobilize us. Yet as soon as we lose our nerve about ourselves, we take cover. Adam and Eve hid, and we all, in one way or another, have used them as role models. Why? Because we do not like what we see. It is uncomfortable—intolerable—to confront our true selves. Simon Tugwell, in his book *The Beatitudes*, explains.

> *And so, like runaway slaves, we either flee our own reality or manufacture a false self which is mostly admirable, mildly prepossessing, and superficially happy. We hide what we know or feel ourselves to be (which we assume to be unacceptable and unlovable) behind some kind of appearance which we hope will be more pleasing. We hide behind pretty faces which we put on for the benefit of our public. And in time we may even come to forget that we are hiding, and think that our assumed pretty face is what we really look like.*[6]

But God loves who we really are—whether we like it or not. God calls us, as He did Adam, to come out of hiding. No amount of spiritual makeup can render us more presentable to Him. As Merton said, "We never make this real, serious return to the center of our own nothingness before God. Hence we never enter into the deepest reality of our relationship with him."[7] His love, which called us into existence, calls us to come out of self-hatred and to step into His truth. "Come to me *now*," Jesus says. "Acknowledge and accept who I want to be for you: a Savior of boundless compassion, infinite patience, unbearable forgiveness, and love that keeps no score of wrongs. Quit projecting onto Me your own feelings about yourself. At this moment your life is a bruised reed, and I will not crush it; a smoldering wick, and I will not quench it. *You are in a safe place.*"

One of the most shocking contradictions in the American church is the intense dislike many disciples of Jesus have for themselves. They are more displeased with their own shortcomings than they would ever dream of being with someone else's. They are sick of their own mediocrity and disgusted by their own inconsistency. David Seamands wrote,

Many Christians . . . find themselves defeated by the most powerful psychological weapon that Satan uses against Christians. This weapon has the effectiveness of a deadly missile. Its name? Low self-esteem. Satan's greatest psychological weapon is a gut-level feeling of inferiority, inadequacy, and low self-worth. This feeling shackles many Christians, in spite of wonderful spiritual experiences . . . and knowledge of God's Word. Although they understand their position as sons and daughters of God, they are tied up in knots, bound by a terrible feeling of inferiority, and chained to a deep sense of worthlessness.[8]

The story is often told of a man who made an appointment with the famous psychologist Carl Jung to get help for chronic depression. Jung told him to reduce his fourteen-hour workday to eight, go directly home, and spend the evenings in his study, quiet and all alone. The depressed man went to his study each night, shut the door, read a little Hermann Hesse or Thomas Mann, played a few Chopin études or some Mozart. After weeks of this, he returned to Jung, complaining that he could see no improvement. On learning how the man had spent his time, Jung said, "But you didn't understand. I didn't want you to be with Hesse or Mann or Chopin or Mozart. I wanted you to be completely alone." The man looked terrified and exclaimed, "I can't think of any worse company." Jung replied, "Yet this is the self you inflict on other people fourteen hours a day"[9] (and, Jung might have added, the self you inflict on yourself).

In my experience, self-hatred is the dominant malaise crippling Christians and stifling their growth in the Holy Spirit. The melancholy spirit of Chekhov's plays—"You live badly, my friends"—haunts the American Christian conscience. Negative voices from our family of origin ("You will never amount to anything"), moralizing from the church, and pressure to be successful transform expectant pilgrims en route to the heavenly Jerusalem into a dispirited traveling troupe of brooding Hamlets and frightened Rullers. Alcoholism, workaholism, mounting addictive behaviors, and the escalating suicide rate reflect the magnitude of the problem. Henri Nouwen observed,

> Over the years, I have come to realize that the greatest trap in our life is not success, popularity, or power, but self-rejection. Success, popularity, and power can indeed present a great temptation, but their seductive quality often comes from the way they are part of the much larger temptation to self-rejection. When we have come to believe in the voices that call us worthless and unlovable, then success, popularity, and power are easily perceived as attractive solutions. The real trap, however, is self-rejection. As soon as someone accuses me or criticizes me, as soon as I am rejected, left alone, or abandoned, I find myself thinking, "Well, that proves once again that I am a nobody." . . . [My dark side says,] I am no good . . . I deserve to be pushed aside, forgotten, rejected, and abandoned. Self-rejection is the greatest enemy of the spiritual life because it contradicts the sacred voice that calls us the "Beloved." Being the Beloved constitutes the core truth of our existence.[10] [emphasis added]

We learn to be gentle with ourselves by experiencing the intimate, heartfelt compassion of Jesus. To the extent that we allow the relentless tenderness of Jesus to invade the citadel of self, we are freed from dyspepsia toward ourselves. Christ wants us to alter our attitude toward ourselves and take sides with Him against our own self-evaluation.

In the summer of 1992, I took a significant step on my inward journey. For twenty days I lived in a remote cabin in the Colorado Rockies and made a retreat, combining therapy, silence, and solitude. Early each morning, I met with a psychologist who guided me in awakening repressed memories and feelings from childhood. The remainder of each day I spent alone in the cabin without television, radio, or reading material of any kind.

As the days passed, I realized that I had not been able to *feel* anything since I was eight years old. A traumatic experience with my mother at that time shut down my memory for the next nine years and my feelings for the next five decades.

When I was eight, the impostor, or false self, was born as a defense against pain. The impostor within whispered, *Brennan, don't ever be your real self anymore, because nobody likes you as you are. Invent a new self that everybody will admire and nobody will know.* So I became a good boy—polite, well mannered, unobtrusive, and deferential. I studied hard, scored excellent grades, won a scholarship in high school, and was stalked every waking moment by the terror of abandonment and the sense that nobody was there for me.

I learned that perfect performance brought the recognition and approval I desperately sought. I orbited into an unfeeling zone to keep fear and shame at a safe distance. As my therapist remarked, "All these years there has been a steel trapdoor covering your emotions and denying you access to them." Meanwhile, the impostor I presented for public inspection was nonchalant and carefree.

The great divorce between my head and my heart endured throughout my ministry. For eighteen years I proclaimed the good news of God's passionate, unconditional love—utterly convicted in my head but not feeling it in my heart. I never felt loved. A scene in the movie *Postcards from the Edge* says it all. A Hollywood film star (Meryl Streep) is told by her director (Gene Hackman) what a wonderful life she has had and how any woman would envy what she has accomplished. Streep answers, "Yes, I know. But you know what? I can't feel any of my life. I've never been able to feel my life and all those good things."

On the tenth day of my mountain retreat, my tears erupted into sobbing. As Mary Michael O'Shaughnessy liked to say, "Often breakdowns lead to breakthroughs." (Much of my callousness and invulnerability has come from my refusal to mourn the loss of a soft word and a tender embrace.) Blessed are those who weep and mourn.

As I drained the cup of grief, a remarkable thing happened: In the distance I heard music and dancing. I was the prodigal son limping home—not a spectator but a participant. The impostor faded, and I was in touch with my true self as the returned child of God. My yearning for praise and affirmation receded.

It used to be that I never felt safe with myself unless I was performing flawlessly. My desire to be perfect had transcended my desire for God. Tyrannized by an all-or-nothing mentality, I interpreted weakness as mediocrity and inconsistency as a loss of nerve. I dismissed compassion and self-acceptance as inappropriate responses. My jaded perception of personal failure and inadequacy led to a loss of self-esteem, triggering episodes of mild depression and heavy anxiety.

Unwittingly I had projected onto God my feelings about myself. I felt safe with Him only when I saw myself as noble, generous, and loving, without scars, fears, or tears—*perfect!* Good grief.

But on that radiant morning in a cabin hidden deep in the Colorado Rockies, I came out of hiding. Jesus removed the shroud of perfectionist performance, and now forgiven and free, I ran home. For I knew that I *knew* Someone was there for me. Gripped in the depth of my soul, tears streaming down my cheeks, I internalized and finally felt all the words I had written and spoken about stubborn, unrelenting Love. That morning I understood that the words were but straw compared to the Reality. I leaped from simply being the teacher of God's love to becoming Abba's delight. I said good-bye to feeling frightened and said *shalom* to feeling safe. What does it mean to feel you are in a safe place? That same afternoon I wrote this in my journal:

> *To feel safe is to stop living in my head and sink down into my heart and feel liked and accepted . . . not having to hide anymore and distract myself with books, television, movies, ice cream, shallow conversation . . . staying in the present moment and not escaping into the past or projecting into the future, alert and attentive to the now . . . feeling relaxed and not nervous or jittery . . . no need to impress or dazzle others or draw attention to myself. . . . un-self-conscious, a new way of being with myself,*

a new way of being in the world . . . calm, unafraid, no anxiety about what's going to happen next . . . loved and valued . . . just being together as an end in itself.

But yes, writing about such an experience risks the invention of a new impostor wearing a glossier disguise. I am reminded of the sobering words of Teresa of Avila: "Such experiences are given to the weaker brothers and sisters to fortify their flagging faith." Even attribution to "the grace of God" can be subtle self-aggrandizement because the phrase has virtually become a Christian cliché.

Thomas Merton, the most sought-after spiritual guide of our time, said one day to a fellow monk, "If I make anything out of the fact that I am Thomas Merton, I am dead. . . . And if you make anything out of the fact that you are in charge of the pig barn . . . you are dead." Merton's solution? "Quit keeping score altogether and surrender ourselves with all our sinfulness to God who sees neither the score nor the scorekeeper but only his child redeemed by Christ."[11]

More than six hundred years ago, Julian of Norwich seized this truth with stunning simplicity when she wrote, "Some of us believe that God is almighty and can do everything; and that he is all-wise and may do everything; but that he is all-love and will do everything—there we draw back. As I see it, this ignorance is the greatest of all hindrances to God's lovers."[12]

Yet there is more. Ponder these words of the apostle Paul: "The things which are done in secret are things that people are ashamed even to speak of; but anything exposed by the light will be *illuminated and anything illuminated turns into light*" (Ephesians 5:12-14, emphasis added).

God not only forgives and forgets our shameful deeds but even turns their darkness into light. All things work together for those who love God, "even," Augustine of Hippo added, "our sins."

Thornton Wilder's one-act play *The Angel That Troubled the Waters*, based on John 5:1-4, dramatizes the power of the pool of Bethesda to heal whenever an angel stirred its waters. A physician comes periodically to the pool hoping to be the first in line and longing to be healed of his melancholy. The angel finally appears but blocks the physician just as he is ready to step into the water. The angel tells the physician to draw back, for this moment is not for him. The physician pleads for help in a broken voice, but the angel insists that healing is not intended for him.

The dialogue continues—and then comes the prophetic word from the angel: "Without your wound where would your power be? It is your very remorse that makes your low voice tremble into the hearts of men. The very angels themselves cannot persuade the wretched and blundering children on earth as can one human being broken on the wheels of living. In Love's service only the wounded soldiers can serve. Draw back."

Later, the man who enters the pool first and is healed rejoices in his good fortune. Turning to the physician, he says: "Come with me first, an hour only, to my home. My son is lost in dark thoughts. I—I do not understand him, and only you have ever lifted his mood. Only an hour . . . my daughter since her child has died, sits in the shadow. She will not listen to us."[13]

Christians who remain in hiding continue to live the lie. We deny the reality of our sin. In a futile attempt to erase our past, we deprive the community of our healing gift. If we conceal our wounds out of fear and shame, our inner darkness can neither be illuminated nor become a light for others. We cling to our bad feelings and beat ourselves with the past when what we should do is let go. As Dietrich Bonhoeffer said, guilt is an idol. But when we dare to live as forgiven men and women, we join the wounded healers and draw closer to Jesus.

Henri Nouwen has explored this theme with depth and sensitivity in his classic work *The Wounded Healer*. He tells the story of a rabbi who asked the prophet Elijah when the Messiah would come. Elijah replied that the rabbi should ask the Messiah directly and that he would find Him sitting at the gates of the city. "How shall I know Him?" the rabbi asked. Elijah replied, "He is sitting among the poor covered with wounds. The others unbind all their wounds at the same time and then bind them up again. But he unbinds one at a time and binds it up again, saying to himself, 'Perhaps I shall be needed: if so I must always be ready so as not to delay for a moment.'"[14]

The Suffering Servant of Isaiah recognizes His wounds, lets them show, and makes them available to the community as a source of healing.

The Wounded Healer implies that grace and healing are communicated through the vulnerability of men and women who have been fractured and heartbroken by life. In Love's service, only wounded soldiers can serve.

Alcoholics Anonymous is a community of wounded healers. Psychiatrist James Knight wrote,

These persons have had their lives laid bare and pushed to the brink of destruction by alcoholism and its accompanying problems. When these persons arise from the ashes of the hellfire of addictive bondage, they have an understanding, sensitivity, and willingness to enter into and maintain healing encounters with their fellow alcoholics. In this encounter they cannot and will not permit themselves to forget their brokenness and vulnerability. Their wounds are acknowledged, accepted, and kept visible. Further, their wounds are used to illuminate and stabilize their own lives while they work to bring the healing of sobriety to their alcoholic brothers and sisters, and sometimes to their sons and daughters. The effectiveness of AA's members in the care and treatment of their fellow alcoholics is one of the great success stories of our time, and graphically illustrates the power of wounds, when used creatively, to lighten the burden of pain and suffering.[15] [emphasis added]

Rainer Maria Rilke, in *Letters to a Young Poet*, explained the efficacy of his own gift: "Do not believe that he who seeks to comfort you lives untroubled among the simple and quiet words that sometimes do you good. His life has much difficulty and sadness and remains far behind yours. Were it otherwise he would never have been able to find those words."[16] Rilke's own wounds of pain and sadness made him aware of his inner poverty and created an emptiness that became the free space into which Christ could pour His healing power. Here was an echo of the cry of Paul: "I shall be very happy to make my weaknesses my special boast so that the power of Christ may stay over me" (2 Corinthians 12:9).

My own journey has taught me that only when I feel safe with God do I feel safe with myself. To trust the Abba who *ran* to His wayward son and never asked any questions enables us to trust ourselves at the core.

The decision to come out of hiding is our initiation rite into the healing ministry of Jesus Christ. It brings its own reward. We stand in the Truth that sets us free and live out of the Reality that makes us whole.

On the list of the ten best books I have read in my lifetime is Georges Bernanos's *Diary of a Country Priest*. Since his ordination, the curate had struggled with doubt, fear, anxiety, and insecurity. His last entry in his diary reads, "It's all over now. The strange mistrust I had of myself, of my own being, has flown, I believe for ever. That conflict is done. . . . I am reconciled to myself, to the poor, poor shell of me. How easy it is to hate oneself! True grace is to forget. Yet if pride could die in us, the supreme grace would be to love oneself in all simplicity—as one would love any of those who themselves have suffered and loved in Christ."[17]

· 2 ·

The Impostor

LEONARD ZELIG IS the quintessential *nebbish* (Yiddish for nerd). In Woody Allen's hilarious and thought-provoking film *Zelig,* he is a celebrity nonentity who fits in everywhere because he actually changes his personality to each evolving situation. He rides in a ticker tape parade; he stands between U.S. presidents Herbert Hoover and Calvin Coolidge; he clowns with prizefighter Jack Dempsey; and he talks theater with playwright Eugene O'Neill. When Hitler rallies his supporters at Nuremberg, Leonard is right there on the speakers' platform.

He has no personality of his own, so he assumes whatever strong personalities he meets up with. With the Chinese, he is straight out of China. With rabbis, he miraculously grows a beard and side curls. With psychiatrists, he apes their jargon, strokes his chin with solemn wisdom. At the Vatican, he is part of Pope Pius XI's clerical retinue. In spring training, he wears a Yankee uniform and stands in the on-deck circle to bat after Babe Ruth. He takes on the black skin of a jazz trumpeter, the blubber of a fatty, the profile of a Mohawk Indian. He is a chameleon. He changes color, accent, shape, as the world about him changes. He has no ideas or opinions of his own; he simply conforms. He wants only to be safe, to fit in, to be accepted, to be liked. . . . He is famous for being nobody, a nonperson.[1]

I could dismiss Allen's caricature of the people pleaser, except that I find so much of Leonard Zelig in myself. This radical *poseur* of my egocentric desires wears a thousand masks. My glittering image must be preserved at all costs. My impostor trembles at the prospect of incurring the displeasure and wrath of others. Incapable of direct speech, he hedges, waffles, procrastinates, and remains silent out of fear of rejection. As James Masterson wrote in *The Search for the Real Self*, "The false self plays its deceptive role, ostensibly protecting us but doing so in a way that is programmed to keep us fearful—of being abandoned, losing support, not being able to cope on our own, not being able to *be* alone."[2]

The impostor lives in fear. For years I have prided myself on being punctual. But in the silence and solitude of that Colorado cabin, I learned that my predictable performance was rooted in the fear of human disapproval. Reprimanding voices from authority figures in my childhood are still fixed in my psyche and trigger warnings of rebuke and sanction.

Impostors are preoccupied with acceptance and approval. Because of their suffocating need to please others, they cannot say no with the same confidence with which they say yes. And so they overextend themselves in people, projects, and causes, motivated not by personal commitment but by the fear of not living up to others' expectations.

The false self was born when as children we were not loved well or were rejected or abandoned. John Bradshaw defines codependency as a disease "characterized by a *loss of identity*. To be codependent is to be out of touch with one's feelings, needs, and desires."[3] The impostor is the classic codependent. To gain acceptance and approval, the false self suppresses or camouflages feelings, making emotional honesty impossible. Living out of the false self creates a compulsive desire to present a perfect image to the public so that everybody will admire us and nobody will know us. The impostor's life becomes a perpetual roller coaster ride of elation and depression.

The false self buys into outside experiences to furnish a personal source of meaning. The pursuit of money, power, glamour, sexual prowess, recognition, and status enhances one's self-importance and creates the illusion of success. The impostor is what he *does*.

For many years, I hid from my true self through my performance in ministry. I constructed an identity through sermons, books, and storytelling. I rationalized that if the majority of Christians thought well of me, there was nothing wrong with me. The more I invested in ministerial success, the more real the impostor became.

The impostor prompts us to attach importance to what has no importance, clothing with a false glitter what is least substantial and turning us away from what is real. The false self causes us to live in a world of delusion.

The impostor is a liar.

Our false self stubbornly blinds each of us to the light and the truth of our own emptiness and hollowness. We cannot acknowledge the darkness within. On the contrary, the impostor proclaims his darkness as the most luminous light, varnishing truth and distorting reality. This brings to mind these words from the apostle John: "If we claim to be without sin, we deceive ourselves and the truth is not in us" (1 John 1:8, NIV).

Craving the approbation withheld in childhood, my false self staggers into each day with an insatiable appetite for affirmation. With my cardboard facade intact, I enter a roomful of people preceded by a muted trumpet—"Here I am"—whereas my true self hidden with Christ in God cries, " Oh, there you are!" The impostor bears a distinct resemblance to alcohol for the alcoholic. He is cunning, baffling, and powerful. He is insidious.

In one of Susan Howatch's early novels, *Glittering Images*, the principal protagonist is Charles Ashworth, a brilliant young Anglican theologian who suddenly experiences complete moral collapse. Estranged from his father and longing for his paternal blessing, Ashworth goes to a monastery to meet with his spiritual director, an older man named Jon Darrow. Ashworth is frightened of being exposed as a venal clergyman and a spiritual failure. Cunningly, his impostor intervenes.

> *The thought of abject failure was appalling enough, but the thought of disappointing Darrow was intolerable. In panic I cast around for a solution which would protect me in my vulnerability, and when Darrow returned to my room that evening, the glittering image said to him: "I do wish you'd tell me more about yourself, Father! There's so much I'd like to know." As soon as the words were spoken I felt myself relaxing. This was an infallible technique for acquiring the good-will of older men; I would ask them about their past, I would listen with the ardent interest of the model disciple and I would be rewarded by a gratifying display of paternal benevolence which would be blind to all the faults and failings I was so desperately anxious to conceal. "Tell me about your days in the Navy!" I urged Darrow with all the warmth and charm I could muster, but although I waited with confidence for the response which would anaesthetise my fear of unfitness, Darrow was silent. . . . Another silence fell as I painfully perceived the machinations of my glittering image.*[4]

The impostor is attentive to the size, shape, and color of the bandages that veil my nothingness. The false self persuades me to be preoccupied with my weight. If I binge on a pint of Häagen-Dazs peanut butter vanilla and the scale signals distress the following morning, I am crestfallen. A beautiful day of sunshine beckons, but for the self-absorbed impostor, the bloom is off the rose. I think Jesus smiles at these minor vanities (checking myself out in the storefront window while pretending to look at the merchandise), but they kidnap my attention away from the indwelling God and temporarily rob me of the joy of God's Holy Spirit. Yet the false self rationalizes my preoccupation with my waistline and overall appearance and whispers, *A fat, sloppy image will diminish your credibility in ministry.* Cunning.

I suspect I am not alone here. The narcissistic obsession with weight watching in North America is a formidable ploy of the impostor. Despite the valid and important health factor, the amount of time, energy, and money devoted to acquiring and maintaining a magazine cover's figure is staggering. No snack is unforeseen, no nibble spontaneous, no calorie uncharted, no strawberry left unaccounted. Professional guidance is procured, books and periodicals scrutinized, health spas subsidized, and the merits of the protein diet debated on national television. What is spiritual ecstasy compared to the exquisite pleasure of six-pack abs and a rock-hard butt? To paraphrase Cardinal Wolsey, "Would that I had served my God the way I have watched my waistline!"

The impostor demands to be noticed. His craving for compliments energizes his futile quest for carnal satisfaction. His bandages are his identity. Appearances are everything. He convolutes *esse quam videri* (to be rather than to seem to be) so that "seeming to be" becomes his *modus operandi.*

Midway through reading a newly published book, I noticed that the author had quoted something I had written previously. Instantly I felt a flush of gratification and a rush of self-importance. As I turned to Jesus in prayer and contacted my true self, the ubiquitous impostor was exposed anew.

"Every one of us is shadowed by an illusory person: a false self," Thomas Merton observed. He went on to explain.

This is the man I want myself to be but who cannot exist, because God does not know anything about him. And to be unknown of God is altogether too much privacy. My false and private self is the one who wants to exist outside the reach of God's will and God's love—outside of reality and outside of life. And such a self cannot help but be an illusion. We are not very good at recognizing illusions, least of all the ones we cherish about ourselves—the ones we were born with and which feed the roots of sin. For most people in the world, there is no greater subjective reality than this false self of theirs, which cannot exist. A life devoted to the cult of this shadow is what is called a life of sin.[5]

Merton's notion of sin focuses not primarily on individual sinful acts but on a fundamental option for a life of pretense. "There can only be two basic loves," wrote Augustine, "the love of God unto the forgetfulness of self, or the love of self unto the forgetfulness and denial of God." The fundamental option arises from the *core* of our being and incarnates itself in the specific choices of daily existence—either for the shadow self ruled by egocentric desires or for the true self hidden with Christ in God.

It is helpful to understand that not all human acts proceed from the core of our being. For instance, a husband makes a sincere choice in his marriage vows to love and honor his wife. But one hot summer day, he loses his cool and gets into a blistering argument with her. Yet he does not retract his choice, because the anger arises from the periphery of his personality, not from the depth of his soul. The act does not touch the heart of his existence or represent a total commitment of his person.

Impostors draw their identity not only from achievements but from interpersonal relationships. They want to stand well with people of prominence because that enhances a person's résumé and sense of self-worth.

One lonely night in the Colorado Rockies, I heard this message: *Brennan, you bring your full presence and attention to certain members of the community but offer a diminished presence to others. Those who have stature, wealth, and charisma—those you find interesting or charming or pretty or famous—command your undivided attention, but people you consider plain or dowdy—those of lesser rank performing menial tasks, the unsung and uncelebrated—are not treated with the same regard. This is not a minor matter to me, Brennan. The way you are with others every day, regardless of their status, is the true test of faith.*

Later in the evening as I dozed off, contrasting images danced on the screen of my mind: Carlton Hayes, a magnificently chiseled athlete in his early twenties, six feet three, 185 pounds, bounces on a trampoline flashing an irresistible Crest-white smile. A crowd has gathered. He switches to skipping rope—a dazzling display of coordination, agility, and grace. The onlookers cheer. "Praise God," the athlete shouts.

Meanwhile, Moe, someone from his retinue of attendants, approaches with a glass of Gatorade. In his early fifties, Moe is five feet four and paunchy. He wears a rumpled suit, shirt open at the collar, tie askew. Moe has a thinning sliver of matted hair extending from his temples to the back of his head, where it disappears in a clump of gray-black hair. The little attendant is unshaven. His bulbous jowls and one glass eye cause the spectators' eyes to dart away.

"Pathetic," one man says.

"Just an obsequious, starstruck hanger-on," adds another.

Moe is neither. His heart is buried with Christ in the Father's love. He moves un-self-consciously through the crowd and extends the Gatorade gracefully to the hero. He is as comfortable as a hand in a glove with his servant role (that is how Jesus first revealed Himself to Moe and transformed his life). Moe feels safe with himself.

That night, Carlton Hayes will deliver the main address at the banquet of the Fellowship of Christian Athletes, who are attending from all fifty states. He will also be honored with a Waterford crystal cup as the first eight-time Olympic gold medalist.

Five thousand people gather at the Ritz-Carlton hotel. Glitterati from the worlds of politics, sports, and show business are scattered throughout the room. As Hayes steps to the podium, the crowd is just finishing a sumptuous meal. The speaker's address abounds with references to the power of Christ and unabashed gratitude to God. Hearts are touched; men and women weep unashamedly, then give a standing ovation.

But behind the glossy delivery, Carlton's vacant stare reveals that his words do not inhabit his soul. Stardom has eroded his presence with

Jesus. Intimacy with God has faded into the distance. The whispering of the Spirit has been drowned out by deafening applause.

Buoyed by success and the roar of the crowd, the Olympic hero moves easily from table to table. He ingratiates himself with everyone—from the waiters to the movie stars. Back at the Red Roof Inn, Moe eats his frozen TV dinner alone. He was not invited to the banquet at the Ritz-Carlton because, quite honestly, he just wouldn't fit in. Surely it wouldn't be fitting for a pot-bellied, glass-eyed attendant to pull up a chair with the likes of Ronald Reagan, Charlton Heston, and Arnold Schwarzenegger.

Moe sits down at the table in his room and closes his eyes. The love of the crucified Christ surges within him. His eyes fill with tears. "Thank You, Jesus," he whispers, as he peels the plastic top off his microwaved lasagna. He flips to Psalm 23 in his Bible.

I was in the dream, too. Where did I choose to spend that evening? My impostor rented a tux and we went to the Ritz. The next morning I awoke in the cabin at four a.m., showered and shaved, fixed a cup of coffee, and thumbed through the Scriptures. My eyes fell on a passage in 2 Corinthians: "From now onwards, therefore, we do not judge anyone by the standards of the flesh" (5:16). Ouch! I lug the false self around even in my dreams.

I relate to Charles Ashworth, the character in the Howatch novel, when his spiritual director comments, "Charles, would I be reading too much into your remarks if I deduced that liking and approval are very important to you?"

"Well, of course they're important!" Ashworth exclaims. "Aren't they important to everyone? Isn't that what life's all about? Success is people liking and approving of you. Failure is being rejected. Everyone knows that."[6]

The sad irony is that the impostor cannot experience intimacy in any relationship. His narcissism excludes others. Incapable of intimacy with self and out of touch with his feelings, intuitions, and insight, the impostor is insensitive to the moods, needs, and dreams of others. Reciprocal sharing is impossible. The impostor has built life around achievements, success, busyness, and self-centered activities that bring gratification and praise from others. James Masterson, M.D., stated, "It is the nature of the false self to save us from knowing the truth about our real selves, from penetrating the deeper causes of our unhappiness, from seeing ourselves as we really are—vulnerable, afraid, terrified, and unable to let our real selves emerge."[7]

Why does the impostor settle for life in such a diminished form? First, because repressed memories from childhood that laid the pattern for self-deception are too painful to recall and thus remain carefully concealed. Faint voices from the past stir vague feelings of angry correction and implied abandonment. Masterson's summary is appropriate: "The false self has a highly skilled defensive radar whose purpose is to avoid feelings of rejection although sacrificing the need for intimacy. This system is constructed during the first years of life, when it is important to detect what would elicit the mother's disapproval."[8]

The second reason the impostor settles for less life is plain old cowardice. As a little one, I could justifiably cop a plea and claim that I was powerless and defenseless. But in the autumn of my life, strengthened by so much love and affection and seasoned by endless affirmation, I must painfully acknowledge that I still operate out of a fear-based center. I have been speechless in situations of flagrant injustice. While the impostor has performed superbly, I have assumed a passive role in relationships, stifled creative thinking, denied my real feelings, allowed myself to be intimidated by others, and then rationalized my behavior by persuading myself that the Lord wants me to be an instrument of peace . . . at what price?

Merton said that a life devoted to the shadow is a life of sin. I have sinned in my cowardly refusal—out of fear of rejection—to think, feel, act, respond, and live from my authentic self. Of course, the impostor "argues relentlessly that the root of the problem is minor and should be ignored, that 'mature' men and women would not get so upset over something so trivial, that one's equilibrium should be maintained even if it means placing unreasonable limits on personal hopes and dreams and accepting life in a diminished form."[9]

...

We even refuse to be our true selves with God—and then wonder why we lack intimacy with Him. The deepest desire of our hearts is for union with God. From the first moment of our existence, our most powerful yearning is to fulfill the original purpose of our lives—to see Him more clearly, love Him more dearly, follow Him more nearly, as the old prayer says. We are made for God, and nothing less will really satisfy us.

C. S. Lewis could say that he was "surprised by joy," gripped by a desire that made "everything else that had ever happened . . . insignificant in comparison." Our hearts will ever be restless until they rest in Him. Jeffrey D. Imbach, in *The Recovery of Love*, wrote, "Prayer is essentially the expression of our heart longing for love. It is not so much the listing of our requests but the breathing of our one deepest request, to be united with God as fully as possible."[10]

Have you ever felt baffled by your internal resistance to prayer? By the existential dread of silence, solitude, and being alone with God? By the way you drag yourself out of bed for morning praise, shuffle off to worship with the sacramental slump of the terminally ill, endure nightly prayer with stoic resignation, knowing that "this too shall pass"?

Beware the impostor!

The false self specializes in treacherous disguise. He is the lazy part of self, resisting the effort, asceticism, and discipline that intimacy with God requires. He inspires rationalizations such as "My work is my prayer; I'm too busy; prayer should be spontaneous, so I just pray when I am moved by the Spirit." The false self's lame excuses allow us to maintain the status quo.

The false self dreads being alone, knowing "that if it would become silent within and without, it would discover itself to be nothing. It would be left with nothing but its own nothingness, and to the false self which claims to be everything, such a discovery would be its undoing."[11]

Obviously, the impostor is antsy in prayer. He hungers for excitement, craves some mood-altering experience. He is depressed when deprived of the spotlight. The false self is frustrated because he never hears God's voice. He cannot, since God sees no one there. Prayer is death to every identity that does not come from God. The false self flees silence and solitude because they remind him of death. Author Parker Palmer has stated, "Becoming totally quiet and unreachably alone are two of the signs that life has gone, while activity and lively communication not only signify life but help us evade the prospect that our life will someday cease."[12]

The impostor's frenetic lifestyle cannot bear the inspection of death because it confronts him with this unbearable truth: "There is no substance under the things with which I am clothed. I am hollow, and my structure of pleasures and ambitions has no foundation. I am objectified in them. But they are all destined by their very contingency to be destroyed. And when they are gone there will be nothing left of me but my own nakedness and emptiness and hollowness, to tell me that I am my own mistake."[13]

The vivisection of the impostor's anatomy appears to be a masochistic exercise in self-flagellation. Isn't such morbid introspection self-defeating? Is this really necessary?

I maintain that it is not only necessary but also indispensable for spiritual growth. The impostor must be called out of hiding, accepted, and embraced. He is an integral part of my total self. Whatever is denied cannot be healed. To acknowledge humbly that I often inhabit an unreal world, that I have trivialized my relationship with God, and that I am driven by vain ambition is the first blow in dismantling my glittering image. The honesty and willingness to stare down the false self dynamites the steel trapdoor of self-deception.

Peace lies in acceptance of truth. Any facet of the shadow self that we refuse to embrace becomes the enemy and forces us into defensive postures. As Simon Tugwell wrote, "The discarded pieces of ourselves will rapidly find incarnation in those around us. Not all hostility is due to this, but it is one major factor in our inability to cope with other people, that they represent to us precisely those elements in ourselves which we have refused to acknowledge."[14]

As we come to grips with our own selfishness and stupidity, we make friends with the impostor and accept that we are impoverished and broken and realize that, if we were not, we would be God. The art of gentleness toward ourselves leads to being gentle with others—and is a natural prerequisite for our presence with God in prayer.

Hatred of the impostor is actually self-hatred. The impostor and I constitute one person. Contempt for the false self gives vent to hostility, which manifests itself as general irritability—an irritation at the same faults in others that we hate in ourselves. Self-hatred always results in some form of self-destructive behavior.

Accepting the reality of our sinfulness means accepting our authentic self. Judas could not face his shadow; Peter could. The latter befriended the impostor within; the former raged against him. "Suicide does not happen on a sudden impulse. It is an act that has been rehearsed during years of unconscious punitive behavior patterns."[15]

Years ago, Carl Jung wrote the following:

The acceptance of oneself is the essence of the moral problem and the epitome of a whole outlook upon life. That I feed the hungry, that I forgive an insult, that I love my enemy in the name of Christ—all these are undoubtedly great virtues. What I do unto the least of my brethren, that I do unto Christ. But what if I should discover that the least amongst them all, the poorest of all the beggars, the most impudent of all the offenders, the very enemy himself—that these are within me, and that I myself stand in need of the alms of my own kindness—that I myself am the enemy who must be loved—what then? As a rule, the Christian's attitude is then reversed; there is no longer any question of love or long-suffering; we say to the brother within us "Raca," and condemn and rage against ourselves. We hide it from the world; we refuse to admit ever having met this least among the lowly in ourselves.[16]

When we accept the truth of what we really are and surrender it to Jesus Christ, we are enveloped in peace, whether or not we feel ourselves to be at peace. By that I mean the peace that passes understanding is not a subjective sensation of peace; if we are in Christ, we are in peace even when we feel no peace.

With a graciousness and an understanding of human weakness that only God can exhibit, Jesus liberates us from alienation and self-condemnation and offers each of us a new possibility. He is the Savior who saves us from ourselves. His Word is freedom. The Master says to us,

Burn the old tapes spinning round in your head that bind you up and lock you into a self-centered stereotype. Listen to the new song of salvation written for those who know that they are poor. Let go of your fear of the Father and your dislike of yourself. Remember the play Don Quixote? *The Knight of the Mirrors lied to him when he said, "See yourself as you really are. Discover that you are not a noble knight, but an idiotic scarecrow of a man. Thou art no knight but a foolish pretender. Look in the mirror of reality. Behold things as they really are. What dost thou see? Naught but an aging fool." The father of lies twists the truth and distorts reality. He is the author of cynicism and skepticism, mistrust and despair, sick thinking and self-hatred. But I am the Son of compassion. You belong to Me, and no one will tear you from My hand.*

Jesus discloses God's true feelings toward us. As we turn the pages of the Gospels, we discover that the people Jesus encounters there are you and me. The understanding and compassion He offers them, He also offers you and me.

On the twentieth and last day of my stay in the Colorado Rockies, I wrote this letter:

> *Good morning, Impostor. Surely you are surprised by the cordial greeting. You probably expected, "Hello, you little jerk," since I have hammered you from day one of this retreat. Let me begin by admitting that I have been unreasonable, ungrateful, and unbalanced in my appraisal of you. (Of course, you are aware, puff of smoke, that in addressing you, I am talking to myself. You are not some isolated, impersonal entity living on an asteroid, but a real part of me.)*
>
> *I come to you today not with rod in hand but with an olive branch. When I was a little boy and first knew that no one was there for me, you intervened and showed me where to hide. (In those Depression days of the thirties, you recall, my parents were doing the best they could with what they had just to provide food and shelter.)*
>
> *At that moment in time, you were invaluable. Without your intervention, I would have been overwhelmed by dread and paralyzed by fear. You were there for me and played a crucial, protective role in my development. Thank you.*
>
> *When I was four years old, you taught me how to build a cottage. Remember the game? I would crawl under the covers from the head of the bed to the footrest and pull the sheets, blanket, and pillow over me—actually believing that no one could find me. I felt safe. I'm still amazed at how effectively it worked. My mind would think happy thoughts, and I would spontaneously smile and start to laugh under the covers. We built that cottage together because the world we inhabited was not a friendly place.*

*But in the construction process you taught me how to hide
my real self from everyone and initiated a lifelong process of
concealment, containment, and withdrawal. Your resourcefulness
enabled me to survive. But then your malevolent side appeared
and you started lying to me.* Brennan, *you whispered,* if you
persist in this folly of being yourself, your few long-suffering
friends will hit the bricks, leaving you all alone. Stuff
your feelings, shut down your memories, withhold your
opinions, and develop social graces so you'll fit in wherever
you are.

*And so the elaborate game of pretense and deception began.
Because it worked, I raised no objection. As the years rolled by,
you/I got strokes from a variety of sources. We were elated and
concluded the game must go on.*

*But you needed someone to bridle you and rein you in.
I had neither the perception nor the courage to tame you, so you
continued to rumble like Sherman through Atlanta, gathering
momentum along the way. Your appetite for attention and
affirmation became insatiable. I never confronted you with the
lie because I was deceived myself.*

*The bottom line, my pampered playmate, is that you are
both needy and selfish. You need care, love, and a safe dwelling
place. On this last day in the Rockies, my gift is to take you where,
unknowingly, you have longed to be—into the presence of Jesus.
Your days of running riot are history. From now on, you slow down,
slow very down.*

*In His presence, I notice that you have already begun to shrink.
Wanna know somethin', little guy? You're much more attractive
that way. I am nicknaming you "Pee-Wee." Naturally, you are not
going to roll over suddenly and die. I know you will get disgruntled
at times and start to act out, but the longer you spend time in the
presence of Jesus, the more accustomed you grow to His face, the*

less adulation you will need because you will have discovered for yourself that He is Enough. And in the Presence, you will delight in the discovery of what it means to live by grace and not by performance.

Your friend,
Brennan

·3·

The Beloved

AFTER COLLEGE PROFESSOR William Least Heat-Moon learned that his job was terminated because of declining enrollment and that his wife from whom he was separated was living with another man, he set out to explore the "blue highways"—the backroads of North America.

One morning, while he was eating breakfast in the campus cafeteria at Mississippi College in Clinton, "a crewcut student wearing mesh step-in casuals sat down to a tall stack of pancakes. He was a methodical fellow. After a prayer running almost a minute, he pulled from his briefcase a Bible, reading stand, clips to hold the book open, a green felt-tip, a pink, and yellow; next came a squeeze-bottle of liquid margarine, a bottle of Log Cabin syrup wrapped in plastic, a linen napkin, and one of those little lemony wet-wipes. The whole business looked like the old circus where twelve men get out of a car the size of a trashcan. . . . 'I thought he was going to pull out a Water-Pik and the Ark of the Covenant next.'"[1]

In this sketch, Moon offers a glimpse of the true self—un-self-conscious, unpretentious, immersed in life, absorbed in the present moment, breathing in God as naturally as a fish swimming in water.

Spirituality is not one compartment or sphere of life. Rather, it is a lifestyle: the process of life lived with the vision of faith. Sanctity lies in discovering my true self, moving toward it, and living out of it.

As the years in the monastery passed, Thomas Merton began to see that the highest spiritual development was to be "ordinary," "to become fully a man, in the way few human beings succeed in becoming so simply and naturally themselves . . . the measures of what others might be if society did not distort them with greed or ambition or lust or desperate want."[2]

John Eagan, who died in 1987, was an ordinary man. An unheralded high school teacher in Milwaukee, he spent thirty years ministering with youth. He never wrote a book, appeared on television, converted the masses, or gathered a reputation for holiness. He ate, slept, drank, biked cross-country, roamed through the woods, taught classes, and prayed. And he kept a journal, published shortly after his death. It is the story of an ordinary man whose soul was seduced and ravished by Jesus Christ. The introduction reads, "The point of John's journal is that we our-selves are the greatest obstacle to our own nobility of soul—which is what sanctity means. We judge ourselves unworthy servants, and that judgment becomes a self-fulfilling prophecy. We deem ourselves too inconsiderable to be used even by a God capable of miracles with no more than mud and spit. And thus our false humility shackles an other-wise omnipotent God."[3]

Eagan, a flawed man with salient weaknesses and character defects, learned that brokenness is proper to the human condition, that we must forgive ourselves for being unlovable, inconsistent, incompetent, irri-table, and potbellied, and he knew that his sins could not keep him from God. They had all been redeemed by the blood of Christ. In repen-tance he took his shadow self to the Cross and dared to live as a forgiven man. In Eagan's journey one hears echoes of Merton: "God is asking me, the unworthy, to forget my unworthiness and that of my brothers, and dare to advance in the love which has redeemed and renewed us all in God's likeness. And to laugh, after all, at the preposterous ideas of 'worthiness.'"[4]

Struggling to shrink the illusory self, Eagan pursued a life of contemplative prayer with ruthless fidelity. During his annual, silent eight-day directed retreat, the revelation of his true self hit with sledge-hammer force. On the morning of the sixth day, he was visiting with his spiritual director.

> *That day Bob says again with great clarity, striking the table with his fist: ... "John, this is your call, the way God is calling you. Pray for a deepening of this love, yes, savor the present moment where God is. Indulge the contemplative in you, surrender to it; let it be, search for God. ..."*
>
> *Then he states something that I will ponder for years; he says it very deliberately. I ask him to repeat it so that I can write it down. "John, the heart of it is this: to make the Lord and his immense love for you constitutive of your personal worth.* Define yourself radically as one beloved by God; *God's love for you and his choice of you constitute your worth. Accept that, and let it become the most important thing in your life."*
>
> *We discuss it. The basis of my personal worth is not my possessions, my talents, not esteem of others, reputation ... not kudos of appreciation from parents and kids, not applause, and everyone telling you how important you are to the place. ... I stand anchored now in God before whom I stand naked, this God who tells me "You are my son, my beloved one."*[5] *[emphasis added]*

The ordinary self is the extraordinary self—the inconspicuous nobody who shivers in the cold of winter and sweats in the heat of sum-mer, who wakes up unreconciled to the new day, who sits before a stack of pancakes, weaves through traffic, bangs around in the basement, shops in the supermarket, pulls weeds and rakes up the leaves, makes love and snowballs, flies kites, and listens to the sound of rain on the roof.

While the impostor draws his identity from past achievements and the adulation of others, the true self claims identity in its beloved-ness. We encounter God in the ordinariness of life: not in the search for spiritual highs and extraordinary, mystical experiences, but in our simple presence in life.

Writing to a New York intellectual and close friend, Henri Nouwen stated, "All I want to say to you is, 'You are the Beloved,' and all I hope is that you can hear these words as spoken to you with all the tenderness and force that love can hold. My only desire is to make these words reverberate in every corner of your being—'You are the Beloved.'"[6] Anchored in this reality, our true self needs neither a muted trumpet to herald our arrival nor a gaudy soapbox to rivet attention from others. We give glory to God simply by being ourselves.

God created us for union with Himself: This is the original purpose of our lives. And God is defined as love (1 John 4:16). Living in awareness of our belovedness is the axis around which the Christian life revolves. Being the beloved is our identity, the core of our existence. It is not merely a lofty thought, an inspiring idea, or one name among many. It is the name by which God knows us and the way He relates to us.

As He has said, "If anyone has ears to hear, let him listen to what the Spirit is saying to the churches: to those who prove victorious I will give the hidden manna and a white stone—a stone with a *new name* written on it, known only to the man who receives it" (Revelation 2:17).

If I must seek an identity outside of myself, then the accumulation of wealth, power, and honors allures me. Or I may find my center of gravity in interpersonal relationships. Ironically, the church itself can stroke the impostor by conferring and withholding honors, offering pride of place based on performance, and creating the illusion of status by rank and pecking order. When belonging to an elite group eclipses the love of God, when I draw life and meaning from any source other than my belovedness, I am spiritually dead. When God gets relegated to second place behind any bauble or trinket, I have swapped the pearl of great price for painted fragments of glass.

"'Who am I?' asked Merton, and he responds, 'I am one loved by Christ.'"[7] This is the foundation of the true self. The indispensable

condition for developing and maintaining the awareness of our belovedness is time alone with God. In solitude we tune out the naysaying whispers of our worthlessness and sink down into the mystery of our true
self. Our longing to know who we really are—which is the source of all
our discontent—will never be satisfied until we confront and accept our
solitude. There we discover that the truth of our belovedness is really
true. Our identity rests in God's relentless tenderness for us revealed in
Jesus Christ.

Our controlled frenzy creates the illusion of a well-ordered existence. We move from crisis to crisis, responding to the urgent and
neglecting the essential. We still walk around. We still perform all the
gestures and actions identified as human, but we resemble people carried along on the mechanical sidewalk at an airport. The fire in the belly
dies. We no longer hear what Boris Pasternak called "the inward music"
of our belovedness. Mike Yaconelli, the cofounder of Youth Specialties,
tells about the time when, dejected and demoralized, he trundled off
with his wife, Karla, to Toronto, Canada, to make a five-day retreat at
the L'Arche (the Ark) community. He went hoping to draw inspiration
from the mentally and physically handicapped people who lived there
or find solace in the presence and preaching of Henri Nouwen. Instead,
he found his true self. He tells his story:

> It took only a few hours of silence before I began to hear my soul speaking.
> It only took being alone for a short period of time for me to discover I
> wasn't alone. God had been trying to shout over the noisiness of my life,
> and I couldn't hear Him. But in the stillness and solitude, His whispers
> shouted from my soul, "Michael, I am here. I have been calling you, but
> you haven't been listening. Can you hear me, Michael? I love you. I have
> always loved you. And I have been waiting for you to hear me say that
> to you. But you have been so busy trying to prove to yourself that you are
> loved . . . that you have not heard me."
>   I heard him, and my slumbering soul was filled with the joy of the

prodigal son. My soul was awakened by a loving Father who had been looking and waiting for me. Finally, I accepted my brokenness. . . . I had never come to terms with that. Let me explain. I knew I was broken. I knew I was a sinner. I knew I continually disappointed God, but I could never accept that part of me. It was a part of me that embarrassed me. I continually felt the need to apologize, to run from my weaknesses, to deny who I was and concentrate on what I should be. I was broken, yes, but I was continually trying never to be broken again—or at least to get to the place where I was very seldom broken. . . .

At L'Arche, it became very clear to me that I had totally misunderstood the Christian faith. I came to see that it was in my brokenness, in my powerlessness, in my weakness that Jesus was made strong. It was in the acceptance of my lack of faith that God could give me faith. It was in the embracing of my brokenness that I could identify with others' brokenness. It was my role to identify with others' pain, not relieve it. Ministry was sharing, not dominating; understanding, not theologizing; caring, not fixing.

What does all this mean?

I don't know . . . and to be quite blunt, that is the wrong question. I only know that at certain times in all of our lives, we make an adjustment in the course of our lives. This was one of those times for me. If you were to look at a map of my life, you would not be aware of any noticeable difference other than a slight change in direction. I can only tell you that it feels very different now. There is an anticipation, an electricity about God's presence in my life that I have never experienced before. I can only tell you that for the first time in my life I can hear Jesus whisper to me every day, "Michael, I love you. You are beloved." And for some strange reason, that seems to be enough.[8]

The unperfumed tone of this narrative gives off the scent of a man without pretense. No pious facade, no false modesty. Something changed that wintry night in Toronto. An earthen vessel with feet of clay laid hold of his belovedness. Yaconelli continued to brush his teeth, coif his ragged beard, pull on his pants one leg at a time, and sit eagerly before a tall stack of pancakes, but his soul was suffused with glory. The tenderness of God had battered the defenses Yaconelli had erected. And hope was restored. The future no longer looked ominous. Taken captive by the *now*, Yaconelli had no space left for anxiety about tomorrow. The impostor did return from time to time, but in the desert of the present moment, Yaconelli rested in a safe place.

We are looking not at some spiritual giant of the Christian tradition, but at an ordinary evangelical man who had encountered the God of ordinary people. The God who grabs scalawags and ragamuffins by the scruff of the neck and raises them up to seat them with the princes and princesses of His people.

Is this miracle enough for anybody? Or has the thunder of "God loved the world so much" been so muffled by the roar of religious rhetoric that we are deaf to the word that God could have tender feelings for us?

· · ·

One thing that struck me in reading Yaconelli's *Back Door* column was the simplicity, honesty, and directness of the words. They stand in marked contrast to the gaseous language of the impostors who hide in evasions, equivocations, and obfuscations.

Back in the heyday of my impostor, I wrote a book review for a fellow impostor's first published work. I defended his prose style, saying, "His floridities are merely orotundity. Nevertheless, his unremitting gaseousness has an organic fluidity and turgescence difficult to duplicate and oddly purgative for the reader." See what I mean?

I began a lecture on the eleventh step of the AA program with a story about a man in a crisis who notices and eats a strawberry. I was emphasizing his ability to live in the present moment. Then I launched into what I considered to be a dazzling explanation of the step, an interpretation filled with profound ontological, theological, and spiritual insights.

Later, a woman approached the podium and said to me, "I loved your story about the strawberry." We agreed that one humble strawberry had more power than all my pompous inanities.

The impostor's vocabulary abounds in puffy, colorless, and self-important words. Is it mere coincidence that the gospel lacks self-conscious, empty language? The Gospels contain no trace of junk words, jargon, or meaningful nonsense at all. Unharnessed and untamed, the impostor often sounds like a cross between William Faulkner and the Marx Brothers. His unctuous pronouncements and pontifications are a profusion of half-truths. Because he is the master of disguise, he can easily slip into feigned humility, the attentive listener, the witty raconteur, the intellectual heavy, or the urbane inhabitant of the global village. The false self is skilled at the controlled openness that scrupulously avoids any significant self-disclosure.

Walker Percy captures this evasiveness in a chilling scene from his novel *The Second Coming*: "She spoke with the quietness of people after a storm which had drowned out their voices. What struck him was not sadness or remorse or pity but the wonder of it. How can it be? How can it happen that one day you are young, you marry, and then another day you come to yourself and your life has passed like a dream? They looked at each other curiously and wondered how they could have missed each other, lived in the same house all those years and passed in the halls like ghosts."[9]

Silence is not simply the absence of noise or the shutdown of communication with the outside world, but rather a process of coming to stillness. Silent solitude forges true speech. I'm not speaking of physical isolation; solitude here means being alone with the Alone, experiencing the transcendent Other and growing in awareness of one's identity as the beloved. It is impossible to know another person intimately without spending time together. Silence makes this solitude a reality. It has been said, "Silence is solitude practiced in action."

It is much like the story of the harried executive who went to the desert father and complained about his frustration in prayer, his flawed virtue, and his failed relationships. The hermit listened closely to his visitor's rehearsal of the struggle and disappointments in trying to lead a Christian life. He then went into the dark recesses of his cave and came out with a basin and a pitcher of water.

"Now watch the water as I pour it into the basin," he said. The water splashed on the bottom and against the sides of the container. It was agitated and turbulent. At first the stirred-up water swirled around the inside of the basin; then it gradually began to settle, until finally the small fast ripples evolved into larger swells that oscillated back and forth. Eventually, the surface became so smooth that the visitor could see his face reflected in the placid water. "That is the way it is when you live constantly in the midst of others," said the hermit. "You do not see yourself as you really are because of all the confusion and disturbance. You fail to recognize the divine presence in your life and the consciousness of your belovedness slowly fades."

It takes time for the water to settle. Coming to interior stillness requires waiting. Any attempt to hasten the process only stirs up the water anew.

Guilt feelings may arise immediately. The shadow self insinuates that you are selfish, wasting time, and evading the responsibilities of family, career, ministry, and community. You can ill afford this idle luxury. Theologian Edward Schillebeeckx wrote, "In a revealed religion, silence with God has a value in itself and for its own sake, just because God is God. Failure to recognize the value of mere[ly] being with God, as the beloved, without doing anything, is to gouge the heart out of Christianity."[10]

Silent solitude makes true speech possible and personal. If I am not in touch with my own belovedness, then I cannot touch the sacredness of others. If I am estranged from myself, I am likewise a stranger to others. Experience has taught me that I connect best with others when I connect with the core of myself. When I allow God to liberate me from unhealthy dependence on people, I listen more attentively, love more unselfishly, and am more compassionate and playful. I take myself less seriously, become aware that the breath of the Father is on my face and that my countenance is bright with laughter in the midst of an adventure I thoroughly enjoy.

Conscientiously "wasting" time with God enables me to speak and act from greater strength, to forgive rather than nurse the latest bruise to my wounded ego, to be capable of magnanimity during the petty moments of life. It empowers me to lose myself, at least temporarily, against a greater background than the tableau of my fears and insecurities, to merely be still and know that God is God. Anthony Padovano commented,

> *It means I don't figure out and don't analyze, but I simply lose myself in the thought or the experience of just being alive, of merely being in a community of believers, but focusing on the essence or presence rather than on what kind of pragmatic consequences should follow from that, merely that it's good to be there, even if I don't know where "there" is, or why it's good to be there. Already I have reached a contemplative stillness in my being.*[11]

Being alone with the Alone moves us from what John Henry Newman called rational or notional knowledge to real knowledge. The first means that I know something in a remote, abstract way that never intrudes on my consciousness; the second means I may not know it but I act on it anyway. In *The Waste Land*, T. S. Eliot wrote, "It's bad tonight, my nerves are shattered. Just talk to me. I'll make it through the night." In solitary silence we listen with great attentiveness to the voice that calls us the beloved. God speaks to the deepest reaches of our souls, into our self-hatred and shame, our narcissism, and takes us through the night into the daylight of His truth: "Do not be afraid, for I have redeemed you; I have called you by your name, you are mine. . . . You are precious in my eyes, because you are honoured and I love you. . . . The mountains may depart, the hills be shaken, but my love for you will never leave you and my covenant of peace with you will never be shaken" (Isaiah 43:1,4; 54:10).

Let us pause here. It is God who has called us by name. The God beside whose beauty the Grand Canyon is only a shadow has called us beloved. The God beside whose power the nuclear bomb is nothing has tender feelings for us.

We are plunged into mystery—what Abraham Heschel called "radical amazement."[12] Hushed and trembling, we are creatures in the presence of ineffable Mystery above all creatures and beyond all telling.

The moment of truth has arrived. We are alone with the Alone. The revelation of God's tender feelings for us is not mere dry knowledge. For too long and too often along my journey, I have sought shelter in hand-clapping liturgies and cerebral Scripture studies. I have received knowledge without appreciation, facts without enthusiasm. Yet when the scholarly investigations were over, I was struck by the insignificance of it all. It just didn't seem to matter.

But when the night is bad and my nerves are shattered and Infinity speaks, when God Almighty shares through His Son the depth of His feelings for me, when His love flashes into my soul and when I am over-taken by Mystery, it is *kairos*—the decisive inbreak of God in this saving moment of my personal history. No one can speak for me. Alone, I face a momentous decision. Shivering in the rags of my winter years, either I escape into skepticism and intellectualism, or with radical amazement I surrender in faith to the truth of my belovedness.

At every moment of our existence God offers us this good news. Sadly, many of us continue to cultivate such an artificial identity that the liberating truth of our belovedness fails to break through. So we become grim, fearful, and legalistic. We hide our pettiness and wallow in guilt. We huff and puff to impress God, scramble for brownie points, thrash about trying to fix ourselves, and live the gospel in such a joyless fashion that it has little appeal to nominal Christians and unbelievers searching for truth.

From hound-dog disciples and sour-faced saints, spare us, oh Lord! Frederick Buechner wrote, "Repent and believe in the gospel, Jesus says. Turn around and believe that the good news that we are loved is better than we ever dared hope, and that to believe in that good news, to live out of it and toward it, to be in love with that good news, is of all glad things in this world the gladdest thing of all. Amen, and come, Lord Jesus."[13]

The chorus of voices quoted in this chapter call out to us to claim the grace given to John Eagan: Define yourself radically as one beloved by God. This is the true self. Every other identity is illusion.

·4·

Abba's Child

YEARS AGO, I directed a parish renewal in Clearwater, Florida. The morning after it ended, the pastor invited me to his home for breakfast. Sitting on my plate was an envelope containing a brief note from a member of the church. It brought tears to my eyes: "Dear Brennan: In all my eighty-three years, I have never had an experience like this. During your week of renewal here at Saint Cecelia's, you promised that if we attended each night, our lives would be changed. Mine has. Last week I was terrified at the prospect of dying; tonight I am homesick for the house of my Abba."

A central theme in the personal life of Jesus Christ, which lies at the very heart of the revelation that He is, is His growing intimacy with, trust in, and love of His Abba.

After His birth in Bethlehem, Jesus was raised in Nazareth by Mary and Joseph according to the strict monotheistic tradition of the Jewish community. Like every devout Jew, Jesus prayed the Shema Israel—"Listen, Israel: Yahweh our God is the one Yahweh" (Deuteronomy 6:4)—three times a day. Jesus was surrounded with the Absolute, dominated by the One, the Eternal, the "I Am Who I Am."

In His human journey, Jesus experienced God in a way that no prophet of Israel had ever dreamed or dared. Jesus was indwelt by the Spirit of the Father and spoke to God using a name that would scandalize both the theology and public opinion of Israel. The name that escaped the mouth of the Nazarene carpenter? *Abba.*

Jewish children used this intimate colloquial form of speech in addressing their fathers, and Jesus Himself employed it with His foster father, Joseph. As a term for divinity, however, its use was unprecedented not only in Judaism but also in any of the great world religions. Joachim Jeremias wrote, "Abba, as a way of addressing God, is *ipsissima vox*, an authentic original utterance of Jesus. We are confronted with something new and astounding. Herein lies the great novelty of the gospel."[1] Jesus, the beloved Son, does not hoard this experience for Himself. He invites and calls us to share the same intimate and liberating relationship.

Paul wrote that "those who are led by the Spirit of God are the children of God. The Spirit you received does not make you slaves, so that you live in fear again; rather, the Spirit you received brought about your adoption to sonship. And by him we cry '*Abba,* Father.' The Spirit himself testifies with our spirit that we are God's children" (Romans 8:14-16, NIV).

John, "the disciple Jesus loved," views intimacy with Abba as the primary effect of the Incarnation: "To all who did accept him he gave power to become children of God" (John 1:12). Hadn't John heard Jesus begin His farewell discourse in the Upper Room with these words— "My little children" (13:33)? Thus John exclaims, "Think of the love that the Father has lavished on us, by letting us be called God's children; and that is what we are" (1 John 3:1).

The greatest gift I have ever received from Jesus Christ has been the Abba experience. "No one knows the Son except the Father, just as no one knows the Father except the Son and those to whom the Son chooses to reveal him" (Matthew 11:27). My dignity as Abba's child is my most coherent sense of self. When I seek to fashion a self-image from the adulation of others and the inner voice whispers, *You've arrived; you're a player in the kingdom enterprise,* there is no truth in that self-concept. When I sink into despondency and the inner voice whispers,

You are no good, a fraud, a hypocrite, and a dilettante, there is no truth in any image shaped from that message. As Gerald May noted, "It is important to recognize these self-commentaries for the mind tricks they are. They have nothing to do with our real dignity. How we view ourselves at any given moment may have very little to do with who we really are."[2]

· · ·

During the course of a silent directed retreat, I journaled the following:

Wernersville, Pennsylvania, January 2, 1977—*Outside, it's dark and below zero. That pretty well describes where I'm at inside. The opening night of an eight-day retreat and I'm filled with a sense of uneasiness, restlessness, even dread. Bone weary and lonely. I can't connect two thoughts about God. Have abandoned any attempt at prayer: It seems too artificial. The few words spoken to God are forced and ring hollow in my empty soul. There is no joy being in His presence. An oppressive but vague feeling of guilt stirs within me. Somehow or other I have failed Him. Maybe pride and vanity have blinded me; maybe insensitivity to pain has hardened my heart. Is my life a disappointment to you? Are You grieved by the shallowness of my soul? Whatever, I've lost You through my own fault, and I am powerless to undo it.*

So began my annual retreat. The physical fatigue soon passed, but the spiritual dryness remained. I groaned through two hours of desolate prayer each morning, another two in the afternoon, and two more at night. Always scatterbrained, disoriented, rowing with one oar in the water. I read Scripture. Dust. I paced the floor. Boredom. Tried a biblical commentary. Zilch.

On the afternoon of the fifth day, I went to the chapel at four p.m. and settled into a straight-backed chair to begin "the great stare"—meditation.

For the next thirteen hours, I remained wide awake, motionless, utterly alert. At ten minutes after five the next morning, I left the chapel with one phrase ringing in my head and pounding in my heart: *Live in the wisdom of accepted tenderness.*

Tenderness awakens within the security of knowing we are thoroughly and sincerely liked by someone. The mere presence of that special someone in a crowded room brings an inward sigh of relief and a strong sense of feeling safe. The experience of a warm, caring, affective presence banishes our fears. The defense mechanisms of the impostor—sarcasm, name-dropping, self-righteousness, the need to impress others—fall away. We become more open, real, vulnerable, and affectionate. We grow tender.

One of my favorite stories is about a priest from Detroit named Edward Farrell who went on his two-week summer vacation to Ireland. His one living uncle was about to celebrate his eightieth birthday. On the great day, the priest and his uncle got up before dawn and dressed in silence. They took a walk along the shores of Lake Killarney and stopped to watch the sunrise, standing side by side with not a word exchanged and staring straight at the rising sun. Suddenly the uncle turned and went skipping down the road. He was radiant, beaming, smiling from ear to ear.

His nephew said, "Uncle Seamus, you really look happy."

"I am, lad."

"Want to tell me why?"

His eighty-year-old uncle replied, "Yes, you see, my Abba is very fond of me."

How would you respond if I asked you this question: "Do you honestly believe God likes you, not just loves you because theologically God *has* to love you?" If you could answer with gut-level honesty, "Oh, yes, my Abba is very fond of me," you would experience a serene compassion for yourself that approximates the meaning of tenderness.

"Can a woman forget her nursing child and have no compassion [tenderness] on the son of her womb? Even these may forget, but I will not forget you" (Isaiah 49:15, NASB).

Scripture suggests that the essence of the divine nature is *compassion* and that the heart of God is defined by *tenderness*. "By the tender mercy [compassion] of our God who from on high will bring the rising Sun to visit us, to give light to those who live in darkness and the shadow of death and to guide our feet into the way of peace" (Luke 1:78-79). Richard Foster wrote, "His heart is the most sensitive and tender of all. No act goes unnoticed, no matter how insignificant or small. A cup of cold water is enough to put tears in the eyes of God. Like the proud mother who is thrilled to receive a wilted bouquet of dandelions from her child so God celebrates our feeble expressions of gratitude."[3]

Jesus, for "in his body lives the fullness of divinity" (Colossians 2:9), singularly understands the tenderness and compassion of the Father's heart. Eternally begotten from the Father, He is Abba's Child. Why did Jesus love sinners, ragamuffins, and the rabble who knew nothing of the Law? Because His Abba loved them. He did nothing on His own, but only what His Abba told Him. Through meal sharing, preaching, teaching, and healing, Jesus acted out His understanding of the Father's indiscriminate love—a love that causes His sun to rise on bad men as well as good, and His rain to fall on honest and dishonest men alike (Matthew 5:45).

In these acts of love Jesus created a scandal for devout, religious Palestinian Jews.

> *The absolutely unpardonable thing was not his concern for the sick, the cripples, the lepers, the possessed . . . nor even his partisanship for the poor, humble people. The real trouble was that he got involved with moral failures, with obviously irreligious and immoral people: people morally and politically suspect, so many dubious, obscure, abandoned, hopeless types existing as an eradicable evil on the fringe of every society. This was the real scandal. Did he really have to go so far? . . . What kind of naive and dangerous love is this, which does not know its limits: the frontiers between fellow countrymen and foreigners, party members and non-members, between neighbors and distant people, between honorable and*

*dishonorable callings, between moral and immoral, good and bad people?
As if dissociation were not absolutely necessary here. As if we ought not to
judge in these cases. As if we could always forgive in these circumstances.*[4]

Because the shining sun and the falling rain are given both to those
who love God and to those who reject God, the compassion of the Son
embraces those who are still living in sin. The pharisee lurking within all
of us shuns sinners. Jesus turns toward them with gracious kindness. He
sustains His attention throughout their lives for the sake of their conversion, "which is always possible to the very last moment."[5]

...

The Holy Spirit is the bond of tenderness between the Father and the Son.
Thus, the indwelling Spirit bears the indelible stamp of the compassion of
God, and the heart of the Spirit-filled person overflows with tenderness.
"The love of God has been poured into our hearts by the Holy Spirit which
has been given us" (Romans 5:5). As partakers of the divine nature, the
noblest aspiration and the most demanding task of our lives is to become
like Christ. In this context, Saint Irenaeus wrote that God took on our
humanness so that we might become like God. Across the centuries this
has meant many different things to many different people. If God is viewed
primarily as omniscient, growth in wisdom and knowledge becomes the
foremost priority of human existence. If God is envisioned as all-powerful,
seeking authority in order to influence others is the way to become like
God. If God is perceived as immutable and invulnerable, granite-like con-
sistency and a high threshold for pain is the way of godliness.

The life of Jesus suggests that to be like Abba is to show compassion. Donald Gray expresses it like this: "Jesus reveals in an exceptionally
human life what it is to live a divine life, a compassionate life."[6]

Scripture points to an intimate connection between compassion
and forgiveness. According to Jesus, a distinctive sign of Abba's child

is the willingness to forgive our enemies: "Love your enemies and do good . . . and you will be sons of the Most High, for he himself is kind to the ungrateful and the wicked" (Luke 6:35). In the Lord's Prayer we acknowledge the primary characteristic of Abba's children when we pray, "Forgive us our trespasses as we forgive those who trespass against us." Jesus presents His Abba as the model for our forgiveness: the king in Matthew 18 who forgives a fantastic sum, an unpayable debt—the God who forgives without limit (the meaning of seventy times seven).

God calls His children to a countercultural lifestyle of forgiveness in a world that demands an eye for an eye—and worse. But if loving God is the first commandment, and loving our neighbor proves our love for God, and if it is easy to love those who love us, then loving our enemies must be the filial badge that identifies Abba's children.

The summons to live as forgiven and forgiving children is radically inclusive. It is addressed not only to the wife whose husband forgot their wedding anniversary but also to parents whose child was slaughtered by a drunken driver, to the victims of slanderous accusations and to the poor living in filthy boxes who see the rich drive by in Mercedes, to the sexually molested and to spouses shamed by the unfaithfulness of their partners, to believers who have been terrorized with blasphemous images of an unbiblical deity and to the mother in El Salvador whose daughter's body was returned to her horribly butchered, to elderly couples who lost all their savings because their bankers were thieves and to the woman whose alcoholic husband squandered their inheritance, and to those who are objects of ridicule, discrimination, and prejudice.

The demands of forgiveness are so daunting that they seem humanly impossible. The demands of forgiveness are simply beyond the capacity of ungraced human will. Only reckless confidence in a Source greater than ourselves can empower us to forgive the wounds inflicted by others. In boundary moments such as these there is only one place to go—Calvary.

Stay there for a long time and watch as Abba's Only Begotten dies utterly alone in bloody disgrace. Watch as He breathes forgiveness on

His torturers at the moment of their greatest cruelty and mercilessness. On that lonely hill outside the city wall of old Jerusalem, you will experience the healing power of the dying Lord.

Experientially, the inner healing of the heart is seldom a sudden catharsis or an instant liberation from bitterness, anger, resentment, and hatred. More often it is a gentle growing into oneness with the Crucified who has achieved our peace through His blood on the cross. This may take considerable time because the memories are still so vivid and the hurt is still so deep. But it *will* happen. The crucified Christ is not merely a heroic example to the church: He is the power and wisdom of God, a living force in His present risenness, transforming our lives and enabling us to extend the hand of reconciliation to our enemies.

Understanding triggers the compassion that makes forgiveness possible. Author Stephen Covey recalled an incident while riding the New York City subway one Sunday morning. The few passengers aboard were reading the newspaper or dozing. It was a quiet, almost somnolent ride through the bowels of the Big Apple. Covey was engrossed in reading when a man accompanied by several small children boarded at the next stop. In less than a minute, bedlam erupted. The kids ran up and down the aisle shouting, screaming, and wrestling with one another on the floor. Their father made no attempt to intervene.

The elderly passengers shifted nervously. Stress became distress. Covey waited patiently. Surely the father would do something to restore order: a gentle word of correction, a stern command, some expression of paternal authority—anything. None was forthcoming. Frustration mounted. After an unduly generous pause, Covey turned to the father and said kindly, "Sir, perhaps you could restore order here by telling your children to come back and sit down." "I know I should do something," the man replied. "We just came from the hospital. Their mother died an hour ago. I just don't know what to do."[7]

The heartfelt compassion that hastens forgiveness matures when we discover why our enemy cries.

...

In 1944 *Life* magazine published a photo essay of a foxhunt in Holmes County, Ohio. The foxes lived in the woods and ate mostly mice and crickets, but sometimes also chicken and quail. This, the story explained, "made the brave men of Holmes County angry because they wanted to kill the quail themselves."[8] So one Saturday about six hundred men and women and their children got together and formed a big circle five miles across. They all carried sticks and started walking through the woods and fields, yelling and baying to frighten the foxes, young and old, out of their holes. Inside this diminishing circle the foxes ran to and fro, tired and frightened. Sometimes a fox would, in its anger, dare to snarl back, and it would be killed on the spot for its temerity. Sometimes one would stop in its anguish and try to lick the hand of its tormentor. It, too, would be killed.

Sometimes, the photo showed, other foxes would stop and stay with their own wounded and dying. Finally, as the circle came closer together, down to a few yards across, the remaining foxes went to the center and lay down inside, not knowing what else to do. But the men and women knew what to do. They hit these dying wounded with their clubs until they were dead, or they showed their children how to do it.

This is a true story. *Life* reported and photographed it. It happened for years in Holmes County every weekend.

Today we cringe at such cruelty, yet we have a foxhunt of our own . . . just ask those who are part of the LGBT community. Sadly, too many have wondered if they had any alternative but to go to the center of the circle and lie down and die.

Where are we in that circle? Where are you? Where would Christ be?

Our hearts of stone become hearts of flesh when we learn where the outcast weeps.

Whenever the gospel is invoked to diminish the dignity of any of God's children, then it is time to get rid of the "so-called" gospel in order that we may experience the gospel. Whenever God is invoked to justify prejudice, contempt, and hostility within the body of Christ, then it is time to heed the words of Meister Eckhart: "I pray that I may be quit of God to find God." Our closed human concepts of gospel and God can prevent us from fully experiencing both.

"But what should the Christian posture be toward the gay community?" one evangelical demanded of me.

"In one of Jesus' parables," I replied, "He enjoined us to let the wheat and the weeds grow together. Paul caught this spirit when he wrote in 1 Corinthians, 'There must be no passing of premature judgment. Leave that until the Lord comes.' The sons and daughters of Abba are the most nonjudgmental people. They get along famously with sinners. Remember the passage in Matthew where Jesus says, 'You must therefore be perfect just as your heavenly Father is perfect'? In Luke, the same verse is translated, 'Be compassionate as your heavenly Father is compassionate.' Bible scholars say that these two words, *perfect* and *compassionate*, can be reduced to the same reality. Conclusion: To follow Jesus in His ministry of compassion precisely defines the biblical meaning of being perfect as the heavenly Father is perfect.

"Besides," I continued, "I am reluctant to push God off His judgment seat and take my place there to pronounce on others when I have neither the knowledge nor the authority to judge anyone. No one at this table has ever seen a motive. Therefore, we cannot suspect what inspired the action of another. Remember Paul's words after his discourse in Romans 1. He begins chapter 2, 'So no matter who you are, if you pass judgment you have no excuse. In judging others you condemn yourself, since you behave no differently from those you judge.' I am reminded of a statement by the Russian novelist Leo Tolstoy: 'If the sexual fantasies of the average person were exposed to view, the world would be horrified.'

"Homophobia ranks among the most shameful scandals of my lifetime. It is frightening to see the incessant intolerance, moral absolutism, and unbending dogmatism that prevail when people insist upon taking the religious high ground. Alan Jones noted that 'it is precisely among those who take their spiritual life seriously that the greatest danger lies.'[9] Pious people are as easily victimized by the tyranny of homophobia as anyone else."

My identity as Abba's child is not an abstraction or a tap dance into religiosity. It is the core truth of my existence. Living in the wisdom of accepted tenderness profoundly affects my perception of reality; the way I respond to people and their life situations; how I treat my brothers and sisters from day to day, whether they be Caucasian, African, Asian, or Hispanic; how I react to the sin-scarred wino on the street; how I respond to interruptions from people I dislike. How I deal with ordinary people in their ordinary unbelief on an ordinary day will speak the truth of who I am more poignantly than the pro-life sticker on the bumper of my car.

We are not for life simply because we are warding off death. We are sons and daughters of the Most High and maturing in tenderness to the extent that we are for others—all others—to the extent that no human flesh is strange to us, to the extent that we can touch the hand of another in love, to the extent that for us there are no "others."

This is the unceasing struggle of a lifetime. It is the long and painful process of becoming like Christ in the way I choose to think, speak, and live each day. Henri Nouwen's words are incisive here: "What is required is to become the Beloved in the common places of my daily existence and, bit by bit, to close the gap that exists between what I know myself to be and the countless specific realities of everyday life. Becoming the Beloved is pulling the truth revealed to me from above down into the ordinariness of what I am, in fact, thinking of, talking about, and doing from hour to hour."[10]

The betrayals and infidelities in my life are too numerous to count. I still cling to the illusion that I must be morally impeccable, other people must be sinless, and the one I love must be without human weakness. But whenever I allow anything but tenderness and compassion to dictate my response to life—be it self-righteous anger, moralizing, defensiveness, the pressing need to change others, carping criticism, frustration at others' blindness, a sense of spiritual superiority, a gnawing hunger of vindication—I am alienated from my true self. My identity as Abba's child becomes ambiguous, tentative, and confused.

Our way of being in the world is the way of tenderness. Everything else is illusion, misperception, falsehood.

The compassionate life is neither a sloppy goodwill toward the world nor the plague of what Robert Wicks calls "chronic niceness." It does not insist that a widow become friendly with her husband's murderer. It does not demand that we like everyone. It does not wink at sin and injustice. It does not accept reality indiscriminately—love and lust, Christianity and atheism, Marxism and capitalism.

The way of tenderness avoids blind fanaticism. Instead, it seeks to see with penetrating clarity. The compassion of God in our hearts opens our eyes to the unique worth of each person. "The other is 'ourself'; and we must love him in his sin as we were loved in our sin."[11]

. . .

I grew up in a lily-white neighborhood in Brooklyn, New York. In 1947, when Branch Rickey, president of our beloved Brooklyn Dodgers, broke the color line by inviting Jackie Robinson to play in the major leagues, we summarily branded him "nigger lover," and many of us switched our allegiance to the New York Yankees. Particularly obnoxious to us was the educated, truculent African-American like Malcolm X, who did not know his place and whose voice rose in what I felt was unjustifiable anger as he challenged white supremacy in the face of black beauty, black need, and black excellence. For Irish Catholics, it was the language of stereotype, the American shorthand still raging today—Willie Horton, law and order, welfare cheats—that whips up fear, ignorance, and votes and keeps discussion, dialogue, and minorities circumscribed.

Along with orthodox Christian beliefs, defense mechanisms against loving—like prejudice, bigotry, false beliefs, and racist and homophobic feelings and attitudes—have been programmed into the computer of my brain since my childhood.

The wounds of racism and homophobia from my childhood have not vanished through intellectual enlightenment and spiritual maturity. They are still in me, as complex and deep in my flesh as blood and nerves. I have borne them all my life with varying degrees of consciousness, but always carefully, always with the most delicate consideration for the pain I would feel if I were somehow forced to acknowledge them. But now I am increasingly aware of the opposite compulsion. I want to know as fully and exactly as I can what the wounds are and how much I am suffering from them. And I want to be healed. I want to be free of the wounds myself, and I do not want to pass them on to my children.[12]

I have tried to deny, ignore, or repress racist and homophobic prejudices as utterly unworthy of a minister of the gospel. Moreover, I felt that to acknowledge their existence would give them power. Ironically, denial and repression are in fact what gives them power.

The impostor starts to shrink only when he is acknowledged, embraced, and accepted. The self-acceptance that flows from embracing my core identity as Abba's child enables me to encounter my utter brokenness with uncompromising honesty and complete abandon to the mercy of God. As my friend Sister Barbara Fiand said, "Wholeness is brokenness owned and thereby healed."

...

Homophobia and racism are among the most serious and vexing moral issues of our day, and both church and society seem to limit us to polarized options.

The "anything goes" morality of the religious and political Left is matched by the sanctimonious moralism of the religious and political Right. Uncritical acceptance of any party line is an idolatrous abdication of one's core identity as Abba's child. Neither liberal fairy dust nor conservative hardball addresses human dignity, which is often dressed in rags.

Abba's children find a third option. They are guided by God's Word and by it alone. All religious and political systems, Right and Left alike, are the work of human beings. Abba's children will not sell their birthright for any mess of pottage, conservative or liberal. They hold fast to their freedom in Christ to live the gospel—uncontaminated by cultural dreck, political flotsam, and the filigreed hypocrisies of bullying religion. Those who are bent on handing gays over to the torturers can lay no claim to moral authority over Abba's children. Jesus saw such shadowed figures as the corrupters of the essential nature of religion in His time. Such exclusive and divisive religion is a trackless place, Eden overgrown, a church in which people experience lonely spiritual alienation from their best human instincts.

Buechner wrote, "We have always known what was wrong with us. The malice in us even at our most civilized. Our insincerity, the masks we do our real business behind. The envy, the way other people's luck can sting us like wasps. And all the slander, making such caricatures of each other that we treat each other like caricatures, even when we love each other. All this infantile nonsense and ugliness. 'Put it away!' Peter says. 'Grow up to salvation!' For Christ's sake, grow up."[13]

The command of Jesus to love one another is never circumscribed by the nationality, status, ethnic background, sexual preference, or inherent lovableness of the "other." The other, the one who has a claim on my love, is anyone to whom I am able to respond, as the parable of the Good Samaritan clearly illustrates. "Which of these three, in your opinion, was neighbor to the man who fell in with the robbers?" Jesus asked. The answer came, "The one who treated him with compassion." He said to them, "Go and do the same."

This insistence on the absolutely indiscriminate nature of compassion within the Kingdom is the dominant perspective of almost all of Jesus' teaching.

What is indiscriminate compassion? "Take a look at a rose. Is it possible for the rose to say, 'I shall offer my fragrance to good people and withhold it from bad people'? Or can you imagine a lamp that withholds its rays from a wicked person who seeks to walk in its light? It could only do that by ceasing to be a lamp. And observe how helplessly and indiscriminately a tree gives its shade to everyone, good and bad, young and old, high and low; to animals and humans and every living creature—even to the one who seeks to cut it down. This is the first quality of love—its indiscriminate character."[14]

Awhile back, Roslyn and I took a day off and decided to play in the French Quarter here in New Orleans. We roamed around Jackson Square sampling gumbo, inhaling jambalaya, and finally stopping at the Häagen-Dazs shrine for the *pièce de résistance*—a praline-pecan Creole hot-fudge sundae that induced a short-lived seizure of pleasure.

As we turned the corner on Bourbon Street, a girl with a radiant smile, about twenty-one years old, approached us, pinned a flower on each of our jackets, and asked if we would like to make a donation to support her mission. When I inquired what her mission was, she replied, "The Unification Church."

"Your founder is Doctor Sun Myung Moon, so I guess that means you're a Moonie?"

"Yes," she answered.

In my mind, she had two strikes against her. First, she was a pagan who did not acknowledge Jesus Christ as her Lord and Savior. Second, she was a naive and vulnerable kid who had been brainwashed by a guru and mesmerized by a cult.

"You know something, Susan?" I said. "I deeply admire your integrity and your fidelity to your conscience. You're out here tramping the streets doing what you really believe in. You are a challenge to anyone who claims the name 'Christian.'"

Roslyn reached out and embraced her, and I embraced the two of them.

"Are you Christians?" she asked.

Roslyn said, "Yes."

She lowered her head, and we saw tears falling on the sidewalk. A minute later she said, "I've been on my mission here in the Quarter for eight days now. You're the first Christians who have ever been nice to me. The others have either looked at me with contempt or screamed and told me that I was possessed by a demon. One woman hit me with her Bible."

What makes the kingdom come is heartfelt compassion: a way of tenderness that knows no frontiers, no labels, no compartmentalizing, and no sectarian divisions. Jesus, the human Face of God, invites us to deep reflection on the nature of true discipleship and the radical lifestyle of Abba's child.

·5·

The Pharisee
and the Child

IN HIS BOOK *WHY I AM NOT A CHRISTIAN*, philosopher Bertrand Russell wrote, "The intolerance that spread over the world with the advent of Christianity is one of its most curious features."[1]

History attests that religion and religious people tend to be narrow. Instead of expanding our capacity for life, joy, and mystery, religion often contracts it. As systematic theology advances, the sense of wonder declines. The paradoxes, contradictions, and ambiguities of life are codified, and God Himself is cribbed, cabined, and confined within the pages of a leather-bound book. Instead of a love story, the Bible is viewed as a detailed manual of directions.

The machinations of manipulative religion surface in every encounter between Jesus Christ and the Pharisees. One confrontation is particularly poignant. In order to grasp its full impact, we must trace the Jewish understanding of the Sabbath.

Initially, the Sabbath was first and foremost a memorial of creation. The book of Genesis states, "God saw all that he had made, and indeed it was very good. . . . On the seventh day God completed the work he had been doing. He rested on the seventh day after all the work he had been doing. God blessed the seventh day and made it holy, because on that day he had rested after all his work of creating" (1:31, 2:2-3).

The seventh day celebrates the completion of the work of creation and is holy to the Lord. The Sabbath is a sacred day, set aside for God, consecrating to Him a specific period of time. It is the Jewish memorial day dedicated to the One who said, "I am the LORD, your Holy One, The Creator" (Isaiah 43:15, NASB). The Sabbath was a solemn recognition that God had sovereign rights, a public act of appropriation wherein the believing community acknowledged that they owed their life and being to Another. As the memorial day of creation, the Sabbath meant a worship of adoration and thanksgiving for all God's goodness, for all the Jews were and had. The rest from work was secondary.

A rest from preoccupation with money, pleasure, and all creature comforts meant getting a proper perspective in relation to the Creator. On the Sabbath, Jews reflected and put the events of the past week in a larger context of saying to God, "You are the true Ruler; I am but Your steward." The Sabbath was a day of rigorous honesty and careful con-templation, a day of taking stock, examining the direction of life, and rooting oneself anew in God. The Jew on the Sabbath learned to pray, "Our hearts are restless all week, until today they rest again in Thee." As a memorial of creation, the Jewish Sabbath foreshadowed the Sunday of the New Testament—the memorial of our re-creation in Christ Jesus.

Second, the Sabbath was also a memorial of the covenant. On Mount Sinai, when God gave the two tablets to Moses, He instructed the people, saying, "The sons of Israel are to keep the sabbath, observ-ing it from generation to generation: this is a lasting covenant. Between myself and the sons of Israel the sabbath is a sign for ever" (Exodus 31:16-17). Thus, every Sabbath was a solemn renewal of the covenant between God and His chosen people. The people renewed their dedica-tion to His service. Every Sabbath they rejoiced anew in the promise of God: "If you obey my voice and hold fast to my covenant, you of all the nations shall be my very own, for all the earth is mine. I will count you a kingdom of priests, a consecrated nation" (Exodus 19:5-6).

Once again, rest from work was not the primary focus of the Sabbath observance. It was both supplementary to worship and a form of worship itself. But worship remained the essential element of the Sabbath celebration.

Years later, the prophet Isaiah would speak of the Sabbath as a day of delight. Fasting and mourning were forbidden. Special festive white clothes were to be worn, and joyous music was to permeate the Sabbath observance. Moreover, the feasting was not restricted to the temple. The Sabbath was and still is the great feast of the orthodox Jewish home—so much so that the Sabbath is considered the chief foundation of the remarkably stable home life and close family spirit that has characterized orthodox Jews through the centuries. All the members of the family were to be present along with invited guests, especially the poor, strangers, or travelers. (In Luke 7, we see Jesus, the itinerant preacher, having dinner on the Sabbath in the home of Simon the Pharisee.)

The Sabbath celebration started at sundown Friday with the mother of the family ceremonially lighting the candles. Then the father, after saying grace over a cup of wine, laid his hand on the head of each of his children and solemnly blessed them with a personal prayer. These and many similar paraliturgical gestures not only hallowed the Sabbath but also sanctified the Jewish home, making it a *mikdash me'at*—a miniature sanctuary in which the parents were the priests and the family table was the altar.

Unfortunately, after the Babylonian exile the primary spiritual meaning of the Sabbath had become obscured. Under spiritually bankrupt leadership, a subtle shift in focus took place. The Pharisees, who carried religion like a shield of self-justification and a sword of judgment, installed the cold demands of rule-ridden perfectionism because that approach gave them status and control while reassuring believers that they were marching in lockstep on the road to salvation. The Pharisees falsified the image of God into an eternal, small-minded bookkeeper whose favor could be won only by the scrupulous observance of laws and regulations. Religion became a tool to intimidate and enslave rather than liberate and empower. Jewish believers were instructed to focus their attention on the secondary aspect of the Sabbath—abstention from work.

The joyous celebration of creation and covenant stressed by the prophets disappeared. The Sabbath became a day of legalism. The means had become the end. (Herein lies the genius of legalistic religion—making primary matters secondary and secondary matters primary.) Concurrently what emerged was a jumble of prohibitions and prescriptions that transformed the Sabbath into a heavy burden leading to nervous scrupulosity—the kind of Sabbath Jesus of Nazareth inveighed against so vehemently.

Seventeen centuries later, the hairsplitting pharisaical interpretation of the Sabbath washed ashore in New England. In the Code of Connecticut we read, "No one shall run on the Sabbath Day, or walk in his garden, or elsewhere, except reverently to and from meeting. No one shall travel, cook victuals, make beds, sweep house, cut hair, or shave on the Sabbath. If any man shall kiss his wife, or wife her husband on the Lord's Day, the party in fault shall be punished at the discretion of the court of magistrates."

Paradoxically, what intrudes between God and human beings is our fastidious morality and pseudopiety. It is not the prostitutes and tax collectors who find it most difficult to repent: It is the devout who feel they have no need to repent, secure in not having broken rules on the Sabbath.

Pharisees invest heavily in extrinsic religious gestures, rituals, methods, and techniques, breeding allegedly holy people who are judgmental, mechanical, lifeless, and as intolerant of others as they are of themselves—violent people, the very opposite of holiness and love, "the type of 'spiritual' people who, conscious of their spirituality, then proceed to crucify the Messiah."[2] Jesus did not die at the hands of muggers, rapists, or thugs. He fell into the well-scrubbed hands of deeply religious people, society's most respected members.

...

At that time Jesus took a walk one sabbath day through the
cornfields. His disciples were hungry and began to pick ears of
corn and eat them. The Pharisees noticed it and said to him,
"Look, your disciples are doing something that is forbidden on
the sabbath." But he said to them, "Have you not read what
David did when he and his followers were hungry—how he
went into the house of God and how they ate the loaves of
offering which neither he nor his followers were allowed to eat,
but which were for the priests alone? Or again, have you not
read in the Law that on the sabbath day the Temple priests
break the Sabbath without being blamed for it? Now here,
I tell you, is something greater than the Temple. And if you had
understood the meaning of the words: What I want is mercy,
not sacrifice, *you would not have condemned the blameless. For*
the Son of Man is master of the sabbath." (MATTHEW 12:1-8,
EMPHASIS ADDED)

The stakes are not small here. The Pharisees insist on the overriding
importance of the rule of law. The basic dignity and genuine needs of
human beings are irrelevant. Jesus, however, insisted that law was not
an end in itself but the means to an end: Obedience was the expression
of the love of God and neighbor, and therefore any form of piety that
stood in the way of love stood in the way of God Himself. Such freedom
challenged the Jewish system. Yet Jesus said He had not come to destroy
the Law but to fulfill it. What He offered was not a new law but a new
attitude toward law based on being loving.

The pharisaic spirit flourishes today in those who use the authority
of religion to control others, entangling them in unending spools of
regulations, watching them struggle and refusing to assist. Eugene
Kennedy asserted, "The Pharisees' power rises from the burden they

heap on the backs of sincere Jews; their gratification comes out of the primitive manipulations of people's fears of displeasing their God."[3] The placard held by one Baptist minister proclaiming "God hates fags" is as offensive and degrading as the sign in the window of a southern thrift store in the 1940s: "No dogs or niggers allowed!"

The words of Jesus—"What I want is mercy, not sacrifice"—are addressed to men and women of religion across the boundaries of time. Kennedy commented, "Whoever in history has put the law, the regulation, the tradition ahead of the suffering person stands in the same field of grain [as the Pharisees] smugly making the same accusation against the innocent."[4]

How many lives have been ruined in the name of narrow-minded, intolerant religiosity!

The pharisee's forte in any age is blaming, accusing, and guilt-tripping others. His gift is noticing the speck in another's eye and failing to see the beam in his own. Blinded by his own ambition, the pharisee cannot see his shadow and thus projects it on others. This is his gift, his signature, his most predictable and reliable response.

Several years ago, en route to a friend's sister's funeral, I drove over a bridge observing the fifty-five–miles per hour limit. I spotted a sign ahead that the speed limit returned to sixty-five. I quickly accelerated to seventy and was suddenly flagged down by a policeman. The officer was African-American. I explained that I was hurrying to a funeral. He listened with indifference, checked my license, and gave me a stiff speeding ticket. In my mind I immediately accused him of racism and vindictiveness and blamed him for my probable late arrival at the church. My dormant inner pharisee announced that he was alive and well.

Whenever we place blame, we are looking for a scapegoat for a real dislocation in which we ourselves are implicated. Blame is a defensive substitute for an honest examination of life that seeks personal growth in failure and self-knowledge in mistakes. Thomas Moore stated, "Fundamentally it is a way of averting consciousness of error."[5]

. . .

Pharisaic Judaism comprised a relatively small group of "separated ones" who, almost two centuries before Christ—in order to preserve the Jewish faith from foreign dilution—had given themselves to lives of vigilant observance of the Mosaic Law. "Their lives were one long rehearsal, a symphony orchestra tuning up endlessly by playing tortured variations of the Law."[6]

Before the Jewish exile, when the spirit of the covenant was vibrantly alive, the people felt safe in the shadow of God's love. In the Pharisaic period, as the understanding of the Hebrew Scriptures deteriorated, the Jews felt safe in the shadow of the Law. Obviously, the gospel of grace presented by the Nazarene carpenter was an outrage.

The attitude of the pharisee is that keeping the law enamors him to God. Divine acceptance is secondary and is conditioned by the pharisee's behavior. For Jesus, the circumstance is diametrically opposite. Being accepted, enamored, and loved by God comes first, motivating the disciple to live the law of love. "We are to love, then, because he loved us first" (1 John 4:19).

Suppose a child has never experienced any love from her parents. One day she meets another little girl whose parents shower her with affection. The first says to herself, "I want to be loved like that too. I have never experienced it, but I'm going to earn the love of my mother and father by my good behavior." So to gain the affection of her parents, she brushes her teeth, makes her bed, smiles, minds her p's and q's, never pouts or cries, never expresses a need, and conceals negative feelings.

This is the way of pharisees. They follow the law impeccably in order to induce God's love. The initiative is theirs. Their image of God necessarily locks them into a theology of works. If God is like the insufferable Nurse Ratched in *One Flew Over the Cuckoo's Nest*, eager to find fault with anybody and everybody, the pharisee must pursue a lifestyle that minimizes mistakes. Then, on Judgment Day, he can present God with a perfect slate, and the reluctant Deity will have to accept it. The psychology of the pharisee makes a religion of washing cups and dishes, fasting twice a week, and paying tithes of mint, dill, and cumin very attractive.

What an impossible burden! The struggle to make oneself presentable to a distant and perfectionistic God is exhausting. Legalists can never live up to the expectations they project on God, "for there will always be a new law, and with it a new interpretation, a fresh hair to be split by the keenest ecclesiastical razor."[7]

The pharisee within is the religious face of the impostor. The idealistic, perfectionist, and neurotic self is oppressed by what Alan Jones calls "a terrorist spirituality."[8] A vague uneasiness about ever being in right relationship with God haunts the pharisee's conscience. The compulsion to feel safe with God fuels this neurotic desire for perfection. This compulsive, endless, moralistic self-evaluation makes it impossible to feel accepted before God. His perception of personal failure leads to a precipitous loss of self-esteem and triggers anxiety, fear, and depression.

The pharisee within usurps my true self whenever I prefer appearances to reality, whenever I am afraid of God, whenever I surrender the control of my soul to rules rather than risk living in union with Jesus, when I choose to look good and not be good, when I prefer appearances to reality. I am reminded of the words of Merton: "If I had a message to my contemporaries . . . it was surely this: be anything you like, be madmen, drunks . . . but at all costs avoid one thing: success."[9] Of course Merton is referring to the cult of success, the pharisaic fascination with honor and power, the relentless drive to enhance the image of the impostor in the eyes of admirers. Conversely, when my false humility spurns the pleasure of achievement and scorns compliments and praise, I become proud of my humility, alienated and isolated from real people, and the impostor rides again!

My resident pharisee is never more prominent than when I assume a stance of moral superiority over racists, bigots, and homophobics. I nod approvingly as the preacher lambastes unbelievers, liberals, New Agers, and others outside the fold. No word would be vitriolic enough for his vigorous condemnation of Hollywood, Super Bowl commercials, provocative clothing, and rock 'n' roll.

Yet my library is filled with biblical commentaries and theology books. I attend church regularly and pray daily. I have a crucifix in my home and a cross in my pocket. My life is completely formed and permeated by religion. I abstain from meat on Friday. I give financial support to Christian organizations. I am an evangelist devoted to God and church.

> *Alas for you, scribes and Pharisees, you hypocrites! You who pay*
> *your tithe of mint and dill and cumin and have neglected the*
> *weightier matters of the Law—justice, mercy, good faith . . . You*
> *blind guides! Straining out gnats and swallowing camels! . . .*
> *Alas for you, scribes and Pharisees, you hypocrites! You who are*
> *like whitewashed tombs that look handsome on the outside, but*
> *inside are full of dead men's bones and every kind of corruption.*
> *In the same way you appear to people from the outside like good*
> *honest men, but inside you are full of hypocrisy and lawlessness.*
> (MATTHEW 23:23-24,27-28)

In the parable of the Pharisee and the publican, the Pharisee stands in the temple and prays, "I thank you, God, that I am not grasping, unjust, adulterous like the rest of mankind, and particularly that I am not like this tax collector here. I fast twice a week; I pay tithes on all I get" (Luke 18:11-12).

His prayer indicates the two telltale flaws of the Pharisee. First, he is very conscious of his religiosity and holiness. When he prays, it is only thanks for what he has, not a request for what he has not and is not. His fault is his belief in his faultlessness. He admires himself. The second defect is related to the first: He despises others. He judges and condemns others, because he is convinced that he stands above them. He is a self-righteous man who unrighteously condemns others.

The pharisee who pardons himself is condemned. The tax collector who condemns himself is acquitted. To deny the pharisee within is lethal. It is imperative that we befriend him, dialogue with him, inquire why he must look to sources outside the kingdom for peace and happiness.

At a prayer meeting I attended, a man in his midsixties was the first to speak: "I just want to thank God that I have nothing to repent of today." His wife groaned. What he meant was he had not embezzled, blasphemed, fornicated, or fractured any of the Ten Commandments. He had distanced himself from idolatry, drunkenness, sexual irresponsibility, and similar things; yet he had never broken through into what Paul calls the inner freedom of the children of God.

If we continue to focus solely on the sinner/saint duality in our person and conduct, while ignoring the raging opposition between the pharisee and the child, spiritual growth will come to an abrupt standstill.

...

In sharp contrast to the pharisaic perception of God and religion, the biblical perception of the gospel of grace is that of a child who has never experienced anything but love and who tries to do her best because she is loved. When she makes mistakes, she knows they do not jeopardize the love of her parents. The possibility that her parents might stop loving her if she doesn't clean her room never enters her mind. They may disapprove of her behavior, but their love is not contingent on her performance.

For the pharisee the emphasis is always on personal effort and achievement. The gospel of grace emphasizes the primacy of God's love. The pharisee savors impeccable conduct; the child delights in the relentless tenderness of God.

In response to her sister's question of what she meant "by remaining a little child before the good God," Thérèse of Lisieux said,

It is recognizing one's nothingness, expecting everything from the good God, just as a little child expects everything from its father; it is not getting anxious about anything, not trying to make one's fortune. . . . Being little is also not attributing to oneself the virtues that one practices, as if one believed oneself capable of achieving something, but recognizing that the good God puts this treasure into the hands of his little child for it to make use of it whenever it needs to; but it is always the good God's treasure. Finally it is never being disheartened by one's faults, because children often fall, but they are too little to do themselves much harm.[10]

Parents love a little one before that child makes his or her mark in the world. A mother never holds up her infant to a visiting neighbor with the words, "This is my daughter. She's going to be a lawyer." Therefore, the secure child's accomplishments later in life are not the effort to gain acceptance and approval but the abundant overflow of her sense of being loved. If the pharisee is the religious face of the impostor, the inner child is the religious face of the true self. The child represents my authentic self and the pharisee the unauthentic. Here we find a winsome wedding of depth psychology and spirituality. Psychoanalysis aims to expose clients' neuroses, to move them away from their falseness, lack of authenticity, and pseudosophistication toward a childlike openness to reality, toward what Jesus enjoins us to be: "unless you become like little children."

The inner child is aware of his feelings and uninhibited in their expression; the pharisee edits feelings and makes a stereotyped response to life situations. On Jacqueline Kennedy's first visit to the Vatican, Pope John XXIII asked his secretary of state, Giuseppe Cardinal Montini, what was the proper way to greet the visiting dignitary, wife of the U.S. president. Montini replied, "It would be proper to say 'madame' or 'Mrs. Kennedy.'" The secretary left, and a few minutes later, the first lady stood in the doorway. The pope's eyes lit up. He trundled over, threw his arms around her, and cried, "Jacqueline!"

The child spontaneously expresses emotions; the pharisee carefully represses them. The question is not whether I am an introvert or an extrovert, a sanguine or a subdued personality. The issue is whether I express or repress my genuine feelings. John Powell once said with sadness that as an epitaph for his parents' tombstone he would have been compelled to write, "Here lie two people who never knew one another." His father could never share his feelings, so his mother never got to know him. To open yourself to another person, to stop lying about your loneliness and your fears, to be honest about your affections, and to tell others how much they mean to you—this openness is the triumph of the child over the pharisee and a sign of the dynamic presence of the Holy Spirit. "Where the Spirit of the Lord is, there is freedom" (2 Corinthians 3:17).

To ignore, repress, or dismiss our feelings is to fail to listen to the stirrings of the Spirit within our emotional life.[11] Jesus listened. In John's gospel, we are told that Jesus was moved with the deepest emotions (11:33). In the book of Matthew we see that His anger erupted: "Hypocrites! It was you Isaiah meant when he so rightly prophesied: This people honours me only with lip-service, while their hearts are far from me. The worship they offer me is worthless" (15:7-9). He called the crowd to intercessory prayer because "he felt sorry for them because they were harassed and dejected, like sheep without a shepherd" (9:36). When He saw the widow of Nain, "he felt sorry for her. 'Do not cry,' he said" (Luke 7:13). Would her son have been resuscitated to life if Jesus had repressed His feelings?

Grief and frustration spontaneously broke through when "as he drew near and came in sight of the city he shed tears over it and said, 'If you in your turn had only understood on this day the message of peace'" (Luke 19:41). Jesus abandoned all emotional restraint when He roared, "The devil is your father, and you prefer to do what your father wants" (John 8:44). We hear more than a hint of irritation when, dining at Simon's house in Bethany, Jesus said, "Leave her alone. Why are you upsetting her?" (Mark 14:6). We hear utter frustration in the words,

"How much longer must I be with you?" (Matthew 17:17), unmitigated rage in "Get behind me, Satan! You are an obstacle in my path" (16:23), extraordinary sensitivity in "Somebody touched me. I felt that power had gone out from me" (Luke 8:46), and blazing wrath in "Take all this out of here and stop turning my Father's house into a market" (John 2:16).

We have spread so many ashes over the historical Jesus that we scarcely feel the glow of His presence anymore. He is a man in a way that we have forgotten men can be: truthful, blunt, emotional, non-manipulative, sensitive, compassionate—His inner child so liberated that He did not feel it unmanly to cry. He met people head on and refused to cut any deal at the price of His integrity. The gospel portrait of the beloved Child of Abba is that of a man exquisitely attuned to His emotions and uninhibited in expressing them. The Son of Man did not scorn or reject feelings as fickle and unreliable. They were sensitive emotional antennae to which He listened carefully and through which He perceived the will of His Father for congruent speech and action.

...

Before going out to dinner, my wife, Roslyn, will often say, "I just need a few minutes to put on my face." A pharisee must wear his or her religious face at all times. The pharisee's voracious appetite for attention and admiration compels him to present an edifying image and to avoid mistakes and failure studiously. Uncensored emotions can spell big trouble.

Yet emotions are our most direct reaction to our perception of ourselves and the world around us. Whether positive or negative, feelings put us in touch with our true selves. They are neither good nor bad: They are simply the truth of what is going on within us. What we do with our feelings will determine whether we live lives of honesty or of deceit. When submitted to the discretion of a faith-formed intellect, our emotions serve as trustworthy beacons for appropriate action or inaction. The denial, displacement, and repression of feelings thwarts self-intimacy.

My indwelling pharisee has devised a way to disembowel my true self, deny my humanity, and camouflage my emotions through a fraudulent mental maneuver called "spiritualizing." My mind's clever tap dance into religiosity shields me from my feelings, usually the kind I am afraid of—anger, fear, and guilt. I distance myself from negative emotions, intuitions, and insights with one foot and hopscotch into rococo rationalizations with the other.

I once wanted to say to a bigot, "If you don't cool it, I'm going to choke you and hang you as an ornament on my Christmas tree"; instead, I reasoned to myself, *God has led this unenlightened brother into my life, and his obnoxious manner is no doubt due to childhood trauma. I must love him in spite of everything.* (Who could argue with that? If bigots hate African-Americans, and I hate bigots, what's the difference?) But the plain truth is that I fled my feelings, lacquered them with pious claptrap, responded like a disembodied spirit, and alienated my true self. When a friend says, "I really don't like you anymore. You never listen to me and always make me feel inferior," I do not grieve. Quickly turning away from the heartache, sadness, and rejection I feel, I conclude, *This is God's way of testing me.* When money is scarce and anxiety sets in, I remind myself, *Jesus said, "Do not worry about tomorrow," so this little setback is just His way of finding out what I am made of.*

When we choose our masked self and deny our real feelings, we fail to recognize our human limitations. Our feelings congeal to the point of callousness. Our interactions with people and life situations are inhibited, conventionalized, and artificial. This spiritualizing wears a thousand faces, none justifiable or healthy—disguises that smother the inner child.

...

When Roslyn was a little girl growing up in the tiny hamlet of Columbia, Louisiana (population nine hundred), her playmate on Saturdays was another little girl named Bertha Bee, the daughter of the African-American housekeeper, Ollie. Together they played dolls in the breezeway, made mud pies by the edge of the lake, ate cookies, shared their lives, and built castles in Spain. One Saturday, Bertha Bee failed to show up. She never returned again. Roslyn knew she wasn't sick, injured, or dead because Ollie would have told her. So Roslyn, nine years old, asked her father why Bertha Bee didn't come to play anymore. She has never forgotten his reply: "It is no longer appropriate." The face that a child wears is her own face, and her eyes that look out on the world do not squint to see labels: black/white, Catholic/Protestant, Asian/Latino, gay/straight, capitalist/socialist. Labels create impressions. This person is wealthy, that one is on welfare. This man is brilliant, another is dim-witted. One woman is beautiful, another dowdy.

Impressions form images that become fixed ideas that give birth to prejudices. Anthony De Mello said, "If you are prejudiced, you will see that person from the eye of that prejudice. In other words, you will cease to see this person as a person."[12] The pharisee within spends most of his time reacting to labels, his own and others'.

The story is told of a man who went to the priest and said, "Father, I want you to say a Mass for my dog."

The priest was indignant. "What do you mean, say a Mass for your dog?"

"It's my pet dog," said the man. "I loved that dog, and I'd like you to offer a Mass for him."

"We don't offer Masses for dogs here," the priest said. "You might try the denomination down the street. Ask them if they have a service for you."

As the man was leaving, he said to the priest, "I really loved that dog. I was planning to offer a million-dollar stipend for the Mass."

And the priest said, "Wait a minute. You never told me your dog was Catholic."

...

At this time the disciples came to Jesus and said, "Who is the greatest in the kingdom of heaven?" So he called a little child to

him and set the child in front of them. Then he said, "I tell you
solemnly, unless you change and become like little children you
will never enter the kingdom of heaven. And so, the one who
makes himself as little as this little child is the greatest in the
kingdom of heaven." (MATTHEW 18:1-4)

In the competitive game of one-upmanship, the disciples are driven by the need to be important and significant. They want to be somebody. According to John Shea, "Every time this ambition surfaces, Jesus places a child in their midst or talks about a child."[13]

The sharpness of Jesus' answer in Matthew 18 has not always been appreciated. Jesus says there is no "first" in the kingdom. If you want to be first, become everybody's lackey; return to your childhood and then you will be fit for the first place. Jesus leaves little room for ambition; and He leaves no more room for the exercise of power. "Lackeys and children are not bearers of power."[14]

The power games the pharisee plays, gross or subtle, are directed toward dominating people and situations, thereby increasing prestige, influence, and reputation. The myriad forms of manipulation, control, and passive aggression originate in the power center. Life is a series of shrewd moves and counter moves. The pharisee within has developed a fine radar system attuned to the vibrations of any person or situation that even remotely threatens his position of authority.

What a friend of mine calls "the king-baby syndrome"—the emotional programming that seeks to compensate for the power deficiency we experienced as infants and youngsters—may lead to a preoccupation with status symbols, whether material possessions or cultivating people with economic or political clout. It may motivate a person to accumulate money as a source of power or to acquire knowledge as a means of achieving recognition as an "interesting" individual. The pharisee knows that knowledge can be power in the religious realm. The expert must be consulted before any definitive judgment can be made. This game of one-upmanship prevents the exchange of ideas and introduces a spirit of rivalry and competition that is antithetical to the un-self-consciousness of the child. Anthony De Mello explained, "The first quality that strikes one when one looks into the eyes of a child is its innocence: its lovely inability to lie or wear a mask or pretend to be anything other than what it is."[15]

The power ploys of the pharisee are predictable. However, the will to power is subtle. It may go undetected and therefore unchallenged. The omnivorous pharisee who succeeds in seizing power, collecting disciples, acquiring knowledge, achieving status and prestige, and controlling his world is estranged from the inner child. He grows fearful when an underling swipes his baton, cynical when feedback is negative, paranoid when threatened, worried when anxious, fitful when challenged, and distraught when defeated. The impostor caught up in the power game lives a hollow life with considerable evidence of success on the outside, while he is desolate, unloving, and anxiety ridden on the inside. King-baby seeks to master God rather than be mastered by Him.[16]

The true self is able to preserve childlike innocence through unflagging awareness of the core identity and by steadfast refusal to be intimidated and contaminated by peers "whose lives are spent not in living but in courting applause and admiration; not in blissfully being themselves but in neurotically comparing and competing, striving for those empty things called success and fame even if they can be attained only at the expense of defeating, humiliating, destroying their neighbors."[17]

· · ·

Counselor John Bradshaw, among others, has offered keen insight into the importance of getting in touch with the inner child. In this age of immense sophistication, vast achievement, and jaded sensibilities, the rediscovery of childhood is a wonderful concept and, as William

McNamara pointed out, can only be enjoyed "by unspoiled children, uncanonized saints, undistinguished sages and unemployed clowns."[18]

Unless we reclaim our child, we will have no inner sense of self, and gradually the impostor becomes who we really think we are. Both psychologists and spiritual writers emphasize the importance of getting to know the inner child as best we can and embracing him or her as a lovable and precious part of ourselves. The positive qualities of the child—openness, trusting dependence, playfulness, simplicity, sensitivity to feelings—restrain us from closing ourselves off to new ideas, unprofitable commitments, the surprises of the Spirit, and risky opportunities for growth. The un-self-consciousness of the child keeps us from morbid introspection, endless self-analysis, and the fatal narcissism of spiritual perfectionism.

Yet we cannot stop with returning home to our inner child. As Jeff Imbach has noted, "First of all, if the inner child is all that is found inside, it still leaves one isolated and alone. There is no final intimacy within if all that we are reclaiming is ourselves."[19] When we seek the inner child on our spiritual journey, we discover not only innocence but what Jean Gill called "the child in shadow."[20] The inner shadow child is undisciplined and dangerous, narcissistic and self-willed, mischievous and capable of hurting a puppy or another child. We label these unattractive traits "childish" and either deny them or block them out of our consciousness.

When I got in touch with the shadow side of my childhood, much of it was riddled with fear. I was afraid of my parents, the church, the dark, and myself. In her novel *Saint Maybe*, Anne Tyler spoke for the surrogate father Ian Bedloe: "It seemed that only Ian knew how these children felt: how scary they found every waking minute. Why, being a child at all was scary! Wasn't that what grownups' nightmares so often reflected—the nightmare of running but getting nowhere, the nightmare of the test you hadn't studied for or the play you hadn't rehearsed? Powerlessness, outsiderness. Murmurs over your head about something everyone knows but you."[21]

Our inner child is not an end in itself but a doorway into the depths of our union with our indwelling God, a sinking down into the fullness of the Abba experience, into the vivid awareness that my inner child is Abba's child, held fast by Him, both in light and in shadow. Consider Frederick Buechner's words:

> We are children, perhaps, at the very moment when we know that it is as children that God loves us—not because we have deserved his love and not in spite of our undeserving; not because we try and not because we recognize the futility of our trying; but simply because he has chosen to love us. We are children because he is our father; and all our efforts, fruitful and fruitless, to do good, to speak truth, to understand, are the efforts of children who, for all their precocity, are children still in that before we loved him, he loved us, as children, through Jesus Christ our Lord.[22]

·6·

Present Risenness

STANDING ON A LONDON STREET CORNER, G. K. Chesterton was approached by a newspaper reporter. "Sir, I understand that you recently became a Christian. May I ask you one question?"

"Certainly," replied Chesterton.

"If the risen Christ suddenly appeared at this very moment and stood behind you, what would you do?"

Chesterton looked the reporter squarely in the eye and said, "He is."

Is this a mere figure of speech, wishful thinking, a piece of pious rhetoric? No, this truth is the most real fact about our life; it is our life. The Jesus who walked the roads of Judea and Galilee is the One who stands behind us. The Christ of history is the Christ of faith.

Biblical theology's preoccupation with the Resurrection is not simply apologetic—that is, it is no longer viewed as the proof *par excellence* of the truth of Christianity. Faith means receiving the gospel message as *dynamis*, reshaping us in the image and likeness of God. The gospel reshapes the hearer through the power of Jesus' victory over death. The gospel proclaims a hidden power in the world—the living presence of the risen Christ. It liberates men and women from the slavery that obscures in them the image and likeness of God.

What gives the teaching of Jesus its power? What distinguishes it from the Koran, the teachings of Buddha, the wisdom of Confucius? *The risen Christ does.* For example, if Jesus did not rise, we can safely praise the Sermon on the Mount as a magnificent ethic. If He did, such praise doesn't matter. The sermon becomes a portrait of our ultimate destiny. The transforming force of the Word resides in the risen Lord who stands by it and thereby gives it final and present meaning.

I will say it again: The dynamic power of the gospel flows from the Resurrection. The New Testament writers repeated this: "All I want is to know Christ and the power of his resurrection" (Philippians 3:10).

When through faith we fully accept that Jesus is who He claims to be, we experience the risen Christ.

God raised Jesus. This is the apostolic witness, the heart of the apostolic preaching. Scripture presents only two alternatives: Either you believe in the Resurrection and you believe in Jesus of Nazareth, or you don't believe in the Resurrection and you don't believe in Jesus of Nazareth.

...

For me, the most radical demand of Christian faith lies in summoning the courage to say yes to the present risenness of Jesus Christ. I have been a Christian for more than fifty years, and I have seen the first fervor wear off in the long, undramatic routine of life. I have lived long enough to appreciate that Christianity is lived more in the valley than on the mountaintop, that faith is never doubt-free, and that although God has revealed Himself in creation and in history, the surest way to know Him is, in the words of Thomas Aquinas, as *tamquam ignotum*, as utterly unknowable. No thought can contain Him; no word can express Him. He is beyond anything we can intellectualize or imagine.

My yes to the fullness of divinity embodied in the present risenness of Jesus is scary because it is so personal. In desolation and abandonment, in the death of my father, in loneliness and fear, in the awareness of the resident pharisee, and in the antics of the impostor, *yes* is a bold word not to be taken lightly or spoken frivolously.

This yes is an act of faith—a decisive, wholehearted response of my whole being to the risen Jesus present beside me, before me, around me, and within me; a cry of confidence that my faith in Jesus provides security not only in the face of death but also in the face of a worse threat posed by my own malice; a word that must be said not just once but repeated over and over again in the ever-changing landscape of life.

An awareness of the resurrected Christ banishes meaninglessness— the dreaded sense that all our life experiences are disconnected and use- less. It helps us to see our lives as all of one piece and reveals a design never perceived before.

Do we see these hints of the present risenness of Jesus?

...

The resurrection of Jesus must be experienced as more than a past histori- cal event. Otherwise, "it is robbed of its impact on the present."[1] In his book *True Resurrection*, Anglican theologian H. A. Williams wrote, "That is why for most of the time resurrection means little to us. It is remote and isolated. And that is why for the majority of people it means nothing. . . . People do well to be skeptical of beliefs not anchored in present experience."[2]

On the other hand, if the central saving act of Christian faith is rele- gated to the future with the fervent hope that Christ's resurrection is the pledge of our own and that one day we shall reign with Him in glory, then the risen One is pushed safely out of the present. Limiting the Resurrection either to the past or to the future makes the present risen- ness of Jesus largely irrelevant, safeguards us from interference with the ordinary rounds and daily routine of our lives, and preempts communion *now* with Jesus as a living person.

In other words, the Resurrection needs to be experienced as pres- ent risenness. If we take seriously the word of the risen Christ—"Know

that I am with you always; yes, to the end of time" (Matthew 28:20)—
we should expect that He will be actively present in our lives. If our
faith is alive and luminous, we will be alert to moments, events, and
occasions when the power of resurrection is brought to bear on our
lives. Self-absorbed and inattentive, we fail to notice the subtle ways
in which Jesus is snagging our attention.

William Barry wrote, "We must school ourselves to pay attention to
our experience in order to discern the touch of God, or what the sociolo-
gist Peter Berger calls the 'rumor of angels,' from all the other influences"[3]
(emphasis added). Let me offer a concrete example.

Late one Saturday night, I returned home from a speaking engagement. The message on my answering machine was brief and pointed:
"Frances Brennan is dying and wants to see you."

The next day I flew to Chicago, took a taxi to San Pierre, Indiana, and
arrived at the Little Company of Mary nursing home around nine p.m.
I went up to the fourth floor and asked the night nurse if Mrs. Brennan was
still in her old room. "Yes," she replied, "room 422, straight down the hall."

This ninety-one-year-old woman, who had been a second mother
to me the last forty years, and whose surname I adopted when I legally
changed my first name in 1960, was lying in bed with a nun sitting
beside her and praying softly. "She's been waiting for you," the sister said.

I leaned over the bed, kissed her on the forehead, and said, "I love
you, Ma." She extended her right hand and pointed to her lips. After a
few seconds of uncertainty I sensed what she wanted. With the little
energy she had left in her frail sixty-two-pound body, she pursed her lips
and we kissed three times. Then she smiled. She died a few hours later.

With a heavy heart I drove to Chicago with friends to make the burial
arrangements. I decided to stay at a motel on Cicero Avenue because of
its proximity to Lamb's Funeral Home. After checking in at the desk,
I took the elevator to the fourth floor, walked down the hall, glanced at
the key, and inserted it in the door. Room 422.

Stunned, I dropped my bag on the floor and sank into a soft chair.

There were 161 rooms in the motel. Sheer coincidence? Then, like a bell sounding deep in my soul, these words rose inside me: "Why do you seek the living among the dead?" Outside, a cloud passed and the sunlight burst through the window. "You're alive, Ma!" My face split into a wide grin. "Congratulations, you're home!"

Perhaps, as John Shea suggests, the boundary between this life and the next is more permeable than many think. "There are signs. People find them in the ordinary and in the extraordinary. They are open to argument and refutation, but their impact on the ones who receive them can only be welcomed. They confirm our deepest yet frailest hope: our love for one another that says, 'Thus, thou shalt not die' is not groundless."[4]

My internal skeptic whispers, "Brennan, your cheese is sliding off your cracker." My resurrection faith hears a rumor of angels, and my eyes see a sunlit communiqué from the risen One, whom Saint Augustine said is more intimate with me than I am with myself.

Frederick Buechner wrote about two experiences that may be whispers from the wings, or they may not be whispers from anywhere. He leaves the reader to decide.

One of them happened when I was in a bar at an airport at an unlikely hour. I went there because I hate flying, and a drink makes it easier to get on a plane. There was nobody else in the place, and there were an awful lot of empty barstools on this long bar, and I sat down at one which had, like all the rest, a little menu in front of it with the drink of the day. On the top of the menu was an object—and the object turned out to be a tie clip, and the tie clip had on it the initials C.F.B., which are my initials, and I was actually stunned by it. Just B would have been sort of interesting, F.B. would have been fascinating, and C.F.B., in the right order—the chances of that being a chance I should think would be absolutely astronomical. What it meant to me, what I chose to believe it meant was: You are in the right place, the right errand, the right road at that moment. How absurd and how small, but it's too easy to say that.

And then another one was just a dream I had of a friend that recently died, a very undreamlike dream where he was simply standing in the room and I said: "How nice to see you, I've missed you," and he said: "Yes, I know that," and I said: "Are you really there?" and he said: "You bet I'm really here," and I said: "Can you prove it?" and he said: "Of course I can prove it," and he threw me a little bit of blue string which I caught. It was so real that I woke up. I recounted the dream at breakfast the next morning with my wife and the widow of the man in the dream, and my wife said, "My God, I saw that on the rug this morning," and I knew it wasn't there last night, and I ran up and sure enough, there was a little squibble of blue thread. Well again, either that's nothing—coincidence— or else it's just a little glimpse of the fact that maybe when we talk about the resurrection of the body, there's something to it![5]

In reading the Celtic chronicles years ago, I was struck by the clear vision of faith in the church of Ireland in medieval times. When a young Irish monk saw his cat catch a salmon swimming in shallow water, he cried, "The power of the Lord is in the paw of the cat." The Chronicles tell of the wandering sailor monks of the Atlantic seeing the angels of God and hearing their songs as they rose and fell over the western islands. To the scientific person they were only gulls and gannets, puffins, cormorants, and kittiwakes. "But the monks lived in a world in which everything was a word of God to them, in which the love of God was manifest in accidental signs, nocturnal communiqués, and the ordinary stuff of our pedestrian lives."[6] If the Father of Jesus monitors every sparrow that drops from the sky and every hair that falls from our heads, perhaps it is not beneath His risen Son to dabble in room keys, monogrammed tie clips, and squibbles of thread.

• • •

Faith in the present risenness of Jesus carries with it life-changing implications for the gritty routine of daily life.

For the sake of clarity and cohesion, we must first consider the meaning of Pentecost. Pentecost is not a feast honoring the Holy Spirit. It is a feast of Christ. It has to do with the Jew, Jesus of Nazareth.[7] Pentecost is the feast of Easter shared with the church, the feast of the resurrection power and glory of Jesus Christ communicated to others.

John stated that while Jesus was still on earth "there was no Spirit as yet because Jesus had not yet been glorified" (7:39). Elsewhere in his gospel we read, "It is for your own good that I am going because unless I go, the Advocate will not come to you; but if I do go, I will send him to you" (16:7). Thus, Paul wrote, "The last Adam has become a life-giving spirit" (1 Corinthians 15:45).

The fourth gospel does not set the scene of the gift of the Spirit on the fiftieth day after Easter, but on Easter Day itself: The Spirit is the Easter gift of Jesus the Christ.[8] "In the evening of that same day, the first day of the week. . . . Jesus came and stood among them. He said to them, 'Peace be with you' . . . After saying this he breathed on them and said: 'Receive the Holy Spirit. For those whose sins you forgive, they are forgiven; for those whose sins you retain, they are retained'" (John 20:19,22-23).

In the oldest texts of 2 Corinthians 3:17, the risen Jesus is Himself called *pneuma*, Spirit: "Now this Lord is the Spirit, and where the Spirit of the Lord is, there is freedom."

Remember that Paul's faith in the Resurrection was based not only on the apostolic witness but also on his own experience of the present risenness of Jesus (Acts 9). Christianity is not simply a message but an experience of faith that becomes a message, explicitly offering hope, freedom from bondage, and a new realm of possibility. As Roger Garaudy, the famous communist philosopher, once remarked about the Nazarene, "I do not know much about this man, but I do know that his whole life conveys this one message: 'anyone can at any moment start a new future.'"[9]

The present risenness of Jesus as "life-giving Spirit" means that I can cope with anything. I am not on my own. "I pray that you may realize . . . how vast are the resources of his Spirit available to us." (See Ephesians 1:18-19.) Relying not on my own limited reserves but on the limitless power of the risen Christ, I can stare down not only the impostor and the pharisee, but even the prospect of my impending death. "[Christ] must be king until [God] has put all his enemies under his feet and the last of the enemies to be destroyed is death" (1 Corinthians 15:25-26).

Our hope is inextricably connected with the conscious awareness of present risenness. During a writing session early one morning, for no apparent reason, a pervasive sense of gloom settled in my soul. I stopped writing and sat down to read the early chapters of the manuscript. I got so discouraged I considered abandoning the whole project. I left the house to get the brake tag on the car renewed. The office was closed. I decided I needed exercise. After jogging two miles on the levee, a thunderstorm hurled sheets of rain, and a howling wind almost blew me into the Mississippi River. I sat down in the tall grass, vaguely aware of clinging to a nail-scarred hand. I returned to the office, cold and soaked, only to get a phone call from Roslyn that led to conflict. My feelings were running rampant—frustration, anger, resentment, fear, self-pity, depression. I repeated to myself, "I am not my feelings." No relief. I tried, "This, too, shall pass." It didn't.

At six that night, emotionally drained and physically spent, I plopped down in a soft chair. I began to pray the Jesus prayer: "Lord Jesus Christ, have mercy on me, a sinner," seeking out His life-giving Spirit. Slowly but perceptibly I awakened to His sacred presence. The loneliness continued but grew gentle, the sadness endured but felt light. Anger and resentment vanished.

A hard day, yes. Rattled and unglued, yes. Unable to cope, no.

How does the life-giving Spirit of the risen Lord manifest Himself on days like that? In our willingness to stand fast, our refusal to run away and escape into self-destructive behavior. Resurrection power enables us to engage in the savage confrontation with untamed emotions, to accept the pain, receive it, take it onboard, however acute it may be. And in the process we discover that we are not alone, that we can stand fast in the awareness of present risenness and so become fuller, deeper, richer disciples. We know ourselves to be more than we previously imagined. In the process we not only endure but are also forced to expand the boundaries of who we think we really are.

"The mystery is Christ among you, your hope of glory" (Colossians 1:27). Hope knows that if great trials are avoided, great deeds remain undone, and the possibility of growth into greatness of soul is aborted. Pessimism and defeatism are never the fruit of the life-giving Spirit but rather reveal our unawareness of present risenness.

A single phone call may abruptly alter the tranquil rhythm of our lives. "Your wife was in a serious accident on the beltway. She is in critical condition at the hospital intensive care unit." Or "I hate to be the bearer of bad news, but your son has been arrested for peddling crack cocaine." Or "Your three-year-old daughter was playing with mine by the side of the pool. I just left them alone for a minute, and your daughter . . ."

When tragedy makes its unwelcome appearance and we are deaf to everything but the shriek of our own agony—when courage flies out the window and the world seems to be a hostile, menacing place—it is the hour of our own Gethsemane. No word, however sincere, offers any comfort or consolation. The night is bad. Our minds are numb, our hearts vacant, our nerves shattered. How will we make it through the night? The God of our lonely journey is silent.

And yet it may happen in these most desperate trials of our human existence that beyond any rational explanation, we may feel a nail-scarred hand clutching ours. We are able, as Etty Hillesum, a Dutch Jewess who died in Auschwitz on November 30, 1943, wrote, to "safeguard that little piece of . . . God in ourselves"[10] and not give way to despair. We make it through the night, and darkness gives way to the light of morning. The tragedy radically alters the direction of our lives, but in our vulnerability and defenselessness we experience the power of Jesus in His present risenness.

...

Present risenness unravels the riddle of life.

In Anne Tyler's novel *Saint Maybe*, Ian Bedloe's mother is a Pollyanna living in a red-bow world. Ceaselessly flashing a pasted-on smile, she runs around like Lancelot's horse in four directions at once. But after the sudden death of her oldest son, she has a moment of deep reflection. Driving home with her husband on Sunday morning from the Church of the Second Chance, she says to him,

> *"Our lives have turned so makeshift and second-class, so second-string, so second-fiddle, and everything's been lost. Isn't it amazing that we keep going? That we keep on shopping for clothes and getting hungry and laughing at jokes on TV? When our oldest son is dead and gone and we'll never see him again and our life's in ruins!"*
>
> *"Now, sweetie," he said.*
>
> *"We've had such extraordinary troubles," she said, "and somehow they've turned us ordinary. That's what's so hard to figure. We're not a special family anymore."*
>
> *"Why, sweetie, of course we're special," he said.*
>
> *"We've turned uncertain. We've turned into worriers."*
>
> *"Bee, sweetie."*
>
> *"Isn't it amazing?"*[1]

After this dialogue, Bee gathers herself together and resumes her all-sweetness-and-light way of being.

Treating life as a series of disconnected episodes is a habit deeply rooted in many of us. We discern no pattern in the experiences and events coming from outside ourselves. Life seems as disjointed as the morning news informing us of a drop in the stock market, the rising flood waters in the Midwest, a foiled terrorist plot in New York, the latest way to cut cancer risk, Miss America's wardrobe, and on and on.

The panoply of information, events, emotions, and experiences stuns us into passivity. We seem content to live life as a series of uncoordinated happenings. Visitors drop by, feelings and ideas come and go, birthdays and anniversaries are observed, sickness and loss arrive unannounced, and nothing seems interrelated.

This is particularly true as the years roll by. In what Shakespeare called "the heyday of the blood," life seemed to be more vivid, events seemed to have more meaning, and the crazy quilt pattern of each day seemed to weave a design. Now, a little older, we are less affected—more "philosophical," we like to tell ourselves. We pride ourselves on having learned in the hard school of life to "cut our losses," and we look back on the past with a certain indulgent pity. How simple things seemed back then, how easy the solution to the riddle of life. Now we are wiser, more mature; we have finally begun to see things as they really are.

Without deliberate awareness of the present risenness of Jesus, life is nonsense, all activity useless, all relationships in vain. Apart from the risen Christ, we live in a world of impenetrable mystery and utter obscurity—a world without meaning, a world of shifting phenomena, a world of death, danger, and darkness. A world of inexplicable futility. Nothing is interconnected. Nothing is worth doing, for nothing endures. Nothing is seen beyond appearances. Nothing is heard but echoes dying on the wind. No love can outlast the emotion that produced it. It is all sound and fury, with no ultimate significance.[12]

The dark riddle of life is illuminated in Jesus; the meaning, purpose, and goal of everything that happens to us, and the way to make it all count, can be learned only from the Way, the Truth, and the Life.

Living in the awareness of the risen Jesus is not a trivial pursuit for the bored and lonely or a defense mechanism enabling us to cope with the stress and sorrow of life. It is the key that unlocks the door to grasping the meaning of existence. All day and every day we are being reshaped into the image of Christ. Everything that happens to us is designed to this end. Nothing that exists can exist beyond the pale of His presence

("All things were created through him and for him"—Colossians 1:16), nothing is irrelevant to it, nothing is without significance in it.

Everything that is comes alive in the risen Christ—who, as Chesterton reminded, is standing behind us. Everything—great, small, important, unimportant, distant, and near—has its place, its meaning, and its value. Through union with Him (as Augustine said, He is more intimate with us than we are with ourselves), nothing is wasted, nothing is missing. There is never a moment that does not carry eternal significance—no action that is sterile, no love that lacks fruition, and no prayer that is unheard. "We know that by turning *everything* to their good, God cooperates with all those who love him" (Romans 8:28, emphasis added).

The apparent frustrations of circumstances, seen or unforeseen, of illness, of misunderstandings, even of our own sins, do not thwart the final fulfillment of our lives hidden with Christ in God.

The awareness of present risenness affects the integration of intuition and will, emotion and reason. Less preoccupied with appearances, we are less inclined to change costumes to win approval with each shift of company and circumstance. We are not one person at home, another in the office; one person at church, another in traffic. We do not pass rudderless from one episode to another, idly seeking some distraction to pass the time, remaining stoic to each new emotion, enduring with a shrug of our shoulders when something irks or irritates. Now circumstances feed us, not we them; we use them, not they us. Gradually we become whole and mature persons whose faculties and energies are harmonized and integrated.

· · ·

When Jesus said that whoever saw Him saw the Father, His hearers were shocked beyond belief. For those of us who have heard these words so often, they have lost their shock value. Yet they contain the power to shatter all our projections and false images of God. Jesus affirmed that

He was the incarnation of all the Father's feelings and attitudes toward humankind. God is no other than as He is seen in the person of Jesus—thus Karl Rahner's phrase, "Jesus is the human face of God."

The central miracle of the gospel is not the raising of Lazarus or the multiplication of the loaves or all the dramatic healing stories taken together. The miracle of the gospel is Christ, risen and glorified, who this very moment tracks us, pursues us, abides in us, and offers Himself to us as companion for the journey! God *pazzo d'amore* and *ebro d'amore* ("crazed with love" and "drunk with love"—Catherine of Siena) is embodied in Jesus dwelling within us.[13]

Paul wrote, "We, with our unveiled faces reflecting like mirrors the brightness of the Lord, all grow brighter and brighter as we are turned into the image that we reflect; this is the work of the Lord who is Spirit" (2 Corinthians 3:18). *The Jerusalem Bible* offers four helpful notes here: (1) Unveiled—as Moses had been. (2) Reflecting or contemplating. (3) The brightness of the Lord is the glory of the risen Jesus, being the glory on the face of Christ (4:6). (4) The contemplation of God in Christ gives the Christian a likeness to God (Romans 8:29 and 1 John 3:2).

Paul had the audacity to boast that he had the mind of Christ (1 Corinthians 2:16). His boast was validated by his life. From the moment of his conversion, his entire attention was riveted on the risen Christ. Jesus Himself was a force whose momentum was ceaselessly at work before Paul's eyes (Philippians 3:21). Jesus was a Person whose voice Paul could recognize (2 Corinthians 13:3), who strengthened Paul in his moments of weakness (12:9), who enlightened him and consoled him (2 Corinthians 1:4-5). Driven to desperation by the slanderous charges of false apostles, Paul admitted to visions and revelations from the Lord Jesus (2 Corinthians 12:1). The Person of Jesus revealed the meaning of life and death (Colossians 3:3).

In the novel *To Kill a Mockingbird*, Atticus Finch said, "You never know a man until you stand in his shoes and walk around in them."[14] Paul looked so unflinchingly at himself, others, and the world through the eyes of Jesus that Christ became the ego of the apostle—"I live now not with my own life but with the life of Christ who lives in me" (Galatians 2:20). Didymus of Alexandria said that "Paul was full of Christ."

Contemplation is gazing at the unveiled glory of God in the risen glorified Christ. Contemplative prayer is above all else looking at the person of Jesus.[15] The prayer of simple awareness means we don't have to get anywhere because we are already there. We are simply coming into consciousness that we possess what we seek. Contemplation, defined as looking at Jesus while loving Him, leads not only to intimacy but also to the transformation of the person contemplating.

In Nathaniel Hawthorne's famous short story *The Great Stone Face*, a young boy stares at the face carved in granite and regularly asks tourists in town if they know the identity of the face on the mountain. No one does. Into manhood, midlife, and old age he continues to gaze on the face at every opportunity, until one day a tourist passing through exclaims to the once-young boy who is now a weather-beaten old man, "You are the face on the mountain!" Contemplative awareness of the risen Jesus shapes our resemblance to Him and turns us into the people God intended us to be.

. . .

Present risenness is the impulse to ministry. "When he saw the crowds he felt sorry for them because they were harassed and dejected, like sheep without a shepherd" (Matthew 9:36). This passage of exquisite tenderness offers a remarkable glimpse into the human soul of Jesus. It tells how He feels about human beings. It reveals His way of looking out on the world, His nonjudgmental attitude toward people who were looking for love in wrong places and seeking happiness in wrong pursuits. It is a simple revelation that the heart of Jesus beats the same yesterday, today, and forever.

Every time the Gospels mention that Jesus was moved with deep emotion for people, they show that it led Him to do something—physical or inner healing, deliverance or exorcism, feeding the hungry crowds or intercessory prayer. Above all, it moved Him to dispel distorted images of who He is and who God is, to lead people out of darkness into light. I'm reminded of this messianic prophecy of Isaiah: "He is like a shepherd feeding his flock, gathering lambs in his arms, holding them against his breast and leading to their rest the mother ewe" (40:11).

Jesus' compassion moved Him to tell people the story of God's love. In an idle moment I try to envision what my life would be like if no one had told me the salvation story and no one had taken the time to introduce me to Jesus. If I were not already dead from alcoholism, the impostor would be running wild. As *The Big Book of Alcoholics Anonymous* tells us, self-will runs riot.

I came across a touching story by Herman Wouk narrated in his novel *Inside, Outside*. His hero was recalling when he had become *B'nai Brith*, a son of the covenant, through his bar mitzva at age thirteen. He then relates:

> *The morning after my bar mitzva, I returned with Pop to the synagogue. What a contrast! Gloomy, silent, all but empty; down front, Morris Elfenbein and a few old men putting on prayer shawls and phylacteries . . .*
>
> *If Pop hadn't made the effort I'd have missed the whole point. Anybody can stage a big bar mitzva, given a bundle of money and a boy willing to put up with the drills for the sake of the winging. The backbone of our religion—who knows, perhaps of all religions in this distracted age—is a stubborn handful in a nearly vacant house of worship, carrying it on for just one more working day; out of habit, loyalty, inertia, superstition, sentiment, or possibly true faith; who can be sure which? My father taught me that somber truth. It has stayed with me, so that I still haul myself to synagogues on weekdays, especially when it rains or snows and the minyan looks chancy.*[16]

The Sinai myth, the key to interpreting Hebrew history and to understanding Jewish identity, is kept alive and passed on by a min-yan (quorum) of stubborn old men in an almost deserted synagogue. However muddled their motives and however frustrated they may become by the apathy and indifference of the crowd, they keep telling the story in season and out.

Our impulse to tell the salvation story arises from listening to the heartbeat of the risen Jesus within us. Telling the story does not require that we become ordained ministers or flamboyant street corner preach-ers, nor does it demand that we try to convert people by concussion with one sledgehammer blow of the Bible after another. It simply means we share with others what our lives used to be like, what happened when we met Jesus, and what our lives are like now.

The impostor recoils at the prospect of telling the story because he fears rejection. He is tense and anxious because he must rely on himself; his power is limited by his paltry resources. He dreads failure.

The true self is not cowed into timidity. Buoyed up and carried on by a power greater than one's own, the true self finds basic security in the awareness of the present risenness of Jesus Christ. Jesus, rather than self, is always the indispensable core of ministry. "Cut off from me you can do nothing" (John 15:5). The moment we acknowledge that we are power-less, we enter into the liberating sphere of the risen One, and we are freed from anxiety over the outcome. We tell the story simply because it is the right thing to do. As the Cambridge classicist F. M. Cornford once said, "The only reason for doing the right thing is that it is the right thing to do; all other reasons are reasons for doing something else."[17]

The late Hollywood film director Frank Capra is best remembered for his 1946 movie *It's a Wonderful Life*. The film is a "'fantasy about a man who falls into suicidal despair because he thinks he has accom-plished nothing of value.' He 'is rescued by a guardian angel who shows him, in a gloriously realized dream sequence, how miserable the lives of his town, his friends, his family would have been had he never existed to touch them with his goodness.'"[18]

Perhaps when the final curtain falls, you will have told the story to only one person. God promises that one cup of living water drawn from the Fountain and passed on to another will not go unrewarded.

. . .

Socrates said, "The unexamined life is not worth living." Sustaining ourselves in the awareness of the present risenness of Jesus is a costly decision that requires more courage than intelligence. I notice a tendency in myself to sink into unawareness, to enjoy some things alone, to exclude Christ, to hug certain experiences and relationships to myself. Exacerbated by what someone has called "the agnosticism of inattention"—the lack of personal discipline over media bombardment, shallow reading, sterile conversation, perfunctory prayer, and subjugation of the senses—the awareness of the risen Christ grows dim. Just as the failure to be attentive undermines love, confidence, and communion in a human relationship, so inattention to my true self hidden with Christ in God obscures awareness of the divine relationship. As the old proverb goes, "Thorns and thistles choke the unused path." A once verdant heart becomes a devastated vineyard.

When I shut Jesus out of my consciousness by looking the other way, my heart is touched by the icy finger of agnosticism. My agnosticism does not consist in the denial of a personal God; it is unbelief growing like lichen from my inattention to the sacred presence. The way I spend my time and money and the way I interact with others routinely testifies to the degree of my awareness or unawareness.

In *The Road Less Traveled*, M. Scott Peck wrote, "Without discipline we can solve nothing. With only some discipline we can solve only some problems. With total discipline we can solve all problems."[19]

With the passing of the years, I am growing more convinced that the discipline of awareness of the present risenness of Jesus is intimately linked to the recovery of passion.

·7·

The Recovery of Passion

THE WORD *PASSION* MEANS basically "'to be affected,' and passion is the essential energy of the soul."[1] It seldom strikes us that the capacity to be affected by anything is a source of energy. Yet we find a luminous illustration of this truth in the gospel of Matthew (13:44).

It appears to be just another long day of manual labor in the weary rhythm of time. But suddenly the ox stops and tugs mischievously. The peasant drives his plowshare deeper into the earth than he usually does. He turns over furrow after furrow until he hears the sound of a harsh metallic noise. The ox stops pawing. The man pushes the primitive plow aside.

With his bare hands he furiously digs up the earth. The dirt flies everywhere. At last the peasant spies a handle and lifts a large earthen pot out of the ground. Trembling, he yanks the handle off the pot. He is stunned. He lets out a scream—"Yaaaahh!"—that makes the ox blink.

The heavy pot is filled to the rim with coins and jewels, silver, and gold. He rifles through the treasure, letting the precious coins, the rare earrings, and the sparkling diamonds slip through his fingers. Furtively, the peasant looks around to see if anyone has been watching him. Satisfied that he is alone, he heaps the dirt over the earthen pot, plows a shallow furrow over the surface, lays a large stone at the spot as a marker, and resumes plowing the field.

He is deeply affected by his splendid find. A single thought absorbs him; in fact, it so controls him that he can no longer work undistracted by day or sleep undisturbed by night. The field must become his property!

As a day laborer, it is impossible for him to take possession of the buried treasure. Where can he get the money to buy the field? Caution and discretion fly out the window. He sells everything he owns. He gets a fair price for his hut and the few sheep he has acquired. He turns to relatives, friends, and acquaintances and borrows significant sums. The owner of the field is delighted with the fancy price offered by the purchaser and sells to the peasant without a second thought.

The new owner's wife is apoplectic. His sons are inconsolable. His friends reproach him. His neighbors wag their heads: "He stayed out too long in the sun." Still, they are baffled by his prodigious energy.

The peasant remains unruffled, even joyful, in the face of widespread opposition. He knows he has stumbled on an extraordinarily profitable transaction and rejoices at the thought of the payoff. The treasure— which apparently had been buried in the field for security before the last war, which the owner did not survive—returns a hundredfold on the price he had paid. He pays off all his debts and builds the equivalent of a mansion in Malibu. The lowly peasant is now a man whose fortune is made, envied by his enemies, congratulated by his friends, and secure for the rest of his life.

> *The kingdom of heaven is like treasure hidden in a field*
> *which someone has found; he hides it again, goes off happy,*
> *sells everything he owns and buys the field.* (MATTHEW 13:44)

This parable focuses on joyous discovery of the kingdom. Biblical scholar Joachim Jeremias commented,

> *When that great joy surpassing all measure seizes a man, it carries him*
> *away, penetrates his inmost being, subjugates his mind. All else seems*

*valueless compared to that surpassing worth. No price is too great to pay.
The unreserved surrender of what is most valuable becomes a matter
of course. The decisive thing in the parable is not what the man gives
up, but his reason for doing so—the overwhelming experience of their
discovery. Thus it is with the kingdom of God. The effect of the joyful
news is overpowering; it fills the heart with gladness; it changes the whole
direction of one's life and produces the most wholehearted self-sacrifice.*[2]

Let's transpose the parable of the treasure into a modern key. On July
10, 1993, Leslie Robins, a thirty-year-old high school teacher from Fond
du Lac, Wisconsin, won $111,000,000 (yep, one hundred and eleven
million dollars), the largest lottery jackpot in U.S. history at the time.
Immediately he flew from Wisconsin to Lakeland, Florida, to regroup
with his fiancée, Colleen DeVries. In a newspaper interview, Robins
said, "The first two days we were probably more scared and intimidated
than elated. Overall, things are beginning to die down enough where we
feel comfortable."[3]

Would it be presumptuous to say that Leslie and Colleen have been
"affected" by their good fortune and that the winning of the Powerball
prize awakened passion in their souls? The identical passion of the peasant in the parable?

Robins had 180 days after the drawing to claim the prize. However,
let's suppose that these two Wisconsin natives are rabid sports fans. They
get so engrossed in the Milwaukee Brewers' chase for the American
League pennant and the Green Bay Packers' run for the Super Bowl
that they forget to claim the prize. The 180 days expire, and they lose the
$3.5 million (after taxes) annually for the next twenty years.

What would our verdict be on the young couple? Foolish?

My response would be the same, though tempered with understanding and compassion. I have done that very thing. Their blind ser-
vitude was sports; mine, alcohol. I can relate to their foolishness. They
forfeited a fortune for the Brewers and Packers; I forfeited the treasure

for bourbon and vodka. During those days of sour wine and withered roses when I was stashing whiskey bottles in the bathroom cabinet, the glove compartment, and the geranium pot, I hid from God in the midst of tears and under hollow laughter. All the while I knew the whereabouts of the treasure.

It is one thing to discover the treasure and quite another to claim it as one's own through ruthless determination and tenacious effort.

The paltriness of our lives is largely due to our fascination with the trinkets and trophies of the unreal world that is passing away. Sex, drugs, booze . . . the pursuit of money, pleasure, and power . . . even a little religion—all suppress the awareness of present risenness. Religious dabbling, worldly prestige, or temporary unconsciousness cannot conceal the terrifying absence of meaning in the church and in society, nor can fanaticism, cynicism, or indifference.

Whatever the addiction—be it a smothering relationship, a dysfunctional dependence, or mere laziness—our capacity to be affected by Christ is numbed. Sloth is our refusal to go on the inward journey, a paralysis that results from choosing to protect ourselves from passion.[4] When we are not profoundly affected by the treasure in our grasp, apathy and mediocrity are inevitable. If passion is not to degenerate into nostalgia or sentimentality, it must renew itself at its source.

The treasure is Jesus Christ. He is the kingdom within. As the signature song of the St. Louis Jesuits goes,

We hold a treasure
not made of gold
in earthen vessels
wealth untold.
One treasure only
The Lord, the Christ
in earthen vessels.

...

The story is told of a very pious Jewish couple. They had married with great love, and the love never died. Their greatest hope was to have a child so their love could walk the earth with joy.

Yet there were difficulties. And since they were very pious, they prayed and prayed and prayed. Along with considerable other efforts, lo and behold, the wife conceived. When she conceived, she laughed louder than Sarah laughed when she conceived Isaac. And the child leapt in her womb more joyously than John leapt in the womb of Elizabeth when Mary visited her. And nine months later a delightful little boy came rumbling into the world.

They named him Mordecai. He was rambunctious, zestful, gulping down the days and dreaming through the nights. The sun and the moon were his toys. He grew in age and wisdom and grace, until it was time to go to the synagogue and learn the Word of God.

The night before his studies were to begin, his parents sat Mordecai down and told him how important the Word of God was. They stressed that without the Word of God, Mordecai would be an autumn leaf in the winter's wind. He listened, wide eyed.

Yet the next day he never arrived at the synagogue. Instead he found himself in the woods, swimming in the lake and climbing the trees.

When he came home that night, the news had spread throughout the small village. Everyone knew of his shame. His parents were beside themselves. They did not know what to do.

So they called in the behavior modificationists to modify Mordecai's behavior, until there was no behavior of Mordecai that was not modified. Nevertheless, the next day he found himself in the woods, swimming in the lake and climbing the trees.

So they called in the psychoanalysts, who unblocked Mordecai's blockages, so there were no more blocks for Mordecai to be blocked by.

Nevertheless, he found himself the next day, swimming in the lake and climbing the trees.

His parents grieved for their beloved son. There seemed to be no hope.

At this same time the Great Rabbi visited the village. And the parents said, "Ah! Perhaps the Rabbi." So they took Mordecai to the Rabbi and told him their tale of woe. The Rabbi bellowed, "Leave the boy with me, and I will have a talking with him."

It was bad enough that Mordecai would not go to the synagogue. But to leave their beloved son alone with this lion of a man was terrifying. However, they had come this far, and so they left him.

Now Mordecai stood in the hallway, and the Great Rabbi stood in his parlor. He beckoned, "Boy, come here." Trembling, Mordecai came forward.

And then the Great Rabbi picked him up and held him silently against his heart.

His parents came to get Mordecai, and they took him home. The next day, he went to the synagogue to learn the Word of God. And when he was done, he went to the woods. And the Word of God became one with the words of the woods, which became one with the words of Mordecai. And he swam in the lake. And the Word of God became one with the words of the lake, which became one with the words of Mordecai. And he climbed the trees. And the Word of God became one with the words of the trees, which became one with the words of Mordecai.

And Mordecai himself grew up to become a great man. People who were seized with panic came to him and found peace. People who were without anybody came to him and found communion. People with no exits came to him and found a way out. And when they came to him he said, "I first learned the Word of God when the Great Rabbi held me silently against his heart."[5]

The heart is traditionally understood as the locus of emotions from which strong feelings such as love and hatred arise. However, this narrow description of the heart as the seat of the affections limits it to one dimension of the total self. Obviously this is not all we have in mind when we pray, "God, create a clean heart in me," or what God meant when He spoke through the mouth of Jeremiah, "Deep within them I will plant my Law, writing it on their hearts" (Jeremiah 31:33), or what Jesus meant when He said, "Happy the pure in heart" (Matthew 5:8).

The heart is the symbol we employ to capture the deepest essence of personhood. It symbolizes what lies at the core of our being; it defines irreducibly who we really are. We can know and be known only through revealing the revelation of what is in our heart.

When Mordecai listened to the heartbeat of the Great Rabbi, he heard more than the systole and diastole of a palpitating human organ. He penetrated the Rabbi's consciousness, entered into his subjectivity, and came to know the Rabbi in a way that embraced intellect and emotion—and transcended them. Heart spoke to heart. Consider Blaise Pascal's provocative statement: "The heart has her reasons about which the mind knows nothing."

...

Once, on a five-day silent retreat, I spent the entire time in John's gospel. Whenever a sentence caused my heart to stir, I wrote it out longhand in a journal. The first of many entries was also the last: "The disciple Jesus loved was reclining next to Jesus . . . leaning back on Jesus' breast" (John 13:23,25). We must not hurry past this scene in search of deeper revelation, or we will miss a magnificent insight. John lays his head on the heart of God, on the breast of the Man whom the Council of Nicea defined as "being coequal and consubstantial to the Father . . . God from God, Light from Light, True God from True God." This passage should not be reduced to a historical memory. It can become a personal encounter, radically affecting our understanding of who God is and what our relationship with Jesus is meant to be. God allows a young Jew, reclining in the rags of his twenty-odd years, to listen to His heartbeat!

Have we ever seen the human Jesus at closer range?

Clearly, John was not intimidated by Jesus. He was not afraid of his Lord and Master. The Jesus John knew was not a hooded mystic abstracted by heavenly visions or a spectral face on a holy card with long hair and a flowing robe. John was deeply affected by this sacred Man.

Fearing that I would miss the divinity of Jesus, I distanced myself from His humanity, like an ancient worshiper shielding his eyes from the Holy of Holies. My uneasiness betrays a strange hesitancy of belief, an uncertain apprehension of a remote Deity rather than intimate confidence in a personal Savior.

As John leans back on the breast of Jesus and listens to the heartbeat of the Great Rabbi, he comes to know Him in a way that surpasses mere cognitive knowledge.

What a world of difference lies between *knowing about* someone and *knowing Him!* We may know all about someone—name, place of birth, family of origin, educational background, habits, appearance—but all those vital statistics tell us nothing about the person who lives and loves and walks with God.

In a flash of intuitive understanding, John experiences Jesus as the human face of the God who is love. And in coming to know who the Great Rabbi is, John discovers who *he* is—the disciple Jesus loved. Years later, the evangelist would write, "In love there can be no fear, but fear is driven out by perfect love: because to fear is to expect punishment, and anyone who is afraid is still imperfect in love" (1 John 4:18).

Beatrice Bruteau wrote, "To know the subject, you have to enter inside the subject, enter into that subject's own awareness, that is, have the same awareness yourself in your own subjectivity: 'Let that mind be in you which was also in Christ Jesus'" (Philippians 2:6).[6]

I sense this is what happened in the Upper Room. Not only did the beloved disciple come to know Jesus, but the meaning of all that Jesus had taught suddenly exploded like a starburst. "I first learned the Word of God when the Great Rabbi held me silently against his heart."

For John, the heart of Christianity was not an inherited doctrine but a message born of his own experience. And the message he declared was, "God is love" (1 John 4:16).

Philosopher Bernard Lonergan once noted, "All religious experience at its roots is an experience of an unconditional and unrestricted being in love."[7]

The recovery of passion begins with the recovery of my true self as the beloved. If I find Christ, I will find myself, and if I find my true self, I will find Him. This is the goal and purpose of our lives. John did not believe that Jesus was the most important thing; he believed that Jesus was the only thing. For "the disciple Jesus loved," anything less was not genuine faith.

I believe that the night in the Upper Room was the defining moment of John's life. Some sixty years after Christ's resurrection, the apostle— like an old gold miner panning the stream of his memories—recalled all that had transpired during his three-year association with Jesus. He made pointed reference to that holy night when it all came together, and he affirmed his core identity with these words: "Peter turned and saw the disciple Jesus loved following them—the one who had leaned on his breast at the supper" (John 21:20).

If John were to be asked, "What is your primary identity, your most coherent sense of yourself?" he would not reply, "I am a disciple, an apostle, an evangelist," but "I am the one Jesus loves."

The beloved disciple's intimate encounter with Jesus on Maundy Thursday night did not pass unnoticed in the early church. Offering explicit testimony to John's authorship of the fourth gospel, Irenaeus (circa AD 180) wrote, "Last of all John, too, the disciple of the Lord who leant against his breast, himself brought out a gospel while he was in Ephesus."[8]

To read John 13:23-25 without faith is to read it without profit. To risk the passionate life, we must be "affected" by Jesus as John was; we must engage His experience with our lives rather than with our memories. Until I lay my head on Jesus' breast, listen to His heartbeat, and personally appropriate the Christ experience of John's eyewitness, I have only a *derivative* spirituality. My cunning impostor will borrow John's moment of intimacy and attempt to convey it as if it were my own.

Once I related the story of an old man dying of cancer.[9] The old man's daughter had asked the local priest to come and pray with her father. When the priest arrived, he found the man lying in bed with his head propped up on two pillows and an empty chair beside his bed. The priest assumed that the old fellow had been informed of his visit. "I guess you were expecting me," he said.

"No, who are you?"

"I'm the new associate at your parish," the priest replied. "When I saw the empty chair, I figured you knew I was going to show up."

"Oh yeah, the chair," said the bedridden man. "Would you mind closing the door?"

Puzzled, the priest shut the door. "I've never told anyone this, not even my daughter," said the man, "but all my life I have never known how to pray. At the Sunday Mass, I used to hear the pastor talk about prayer, but it always went right over my head. Finally I said to him one day in sheer frustration, 'I get nothing out of your homilies on prayer.'

"'Here,' says my pastor, reaching into the bottom drawer of his desk. 'Read this book by Hans Urs von Balthasar. He's a Swiss theologian. It's the best book on contemplative prayer in the twentieth century.'

"Well, Father," says the man, "I took the book home and tried to read it. But in the first three pages I had to look up twelve words in the dictionary. I gave the book back to my pastor, thanked him, and under my breath whispered, 'for nothin.'

"I abandoned any attempt at prayer," he continued, "until one day about four years ago my best friend said to me, 'Joe, prayer is just a simple matter of having a conversation with Jesus. Here's what I suggest.

Sit down on a chair, place an empty chair in front of you, and in faith see Jesus on the chair. It's not spooky because He promised, "I'll be with you all days." Then just speak to Him and listen in the same way you're doing with me right now.'

"So, Padre, I tried it, and I've liked it so much that I do it a couple of hours every day. I'm careful, though. If my daughter saw me talking to an empty chair, she'd either have a nervous breakdown or send me off to the funny farm."

The priest was deeply moved by the story and encouraged the old guy to continue on the journey. Then he prayed with him, anointed him with oil, and returned to the rectory.

Two nights later the daughter called to tell the priest that her daddy had died that afternoon.

"Did he seem to die in peace?" he asked.

"Yes, when I left the house around two o'clock, he called me over to his bedside, told me one of his corny jokes, and kissed me on the cheek. When I got back from the store an hour later, I found him dead. But there was something strange, Father. In fact, beyond strange—kinda weird. Apparently just before Daddy died, he leaned over and rested his head on a chair beside his bed."

The Christ of faith is no less accessible to us in His present risenness than was the Christ of history in His human flesh to the beloved disciple. John emphasizes this truth when he quotes the Master: "I tell you the truth, it is to your advantage that I go away" (16:7, NASB). Why? How could Jesus' departure benefit the community of believers? First, "for if I do not go away, the Helper will not come to you; but if I go, I will send Him to you." Second, while Jesus was still visible on earth, there was the danger that the apostles would be so wedded to the sight of His human body that they would trade the certainty of faith for the tangible evidence of the senses. To have seen Jesus in the flesh was an extraordinary privilege, but more blessed are they who have not seen and yet believe (see John 20:29).

...

In the light of John's own experience, it comes as no surprise that he puts but one central question to readers of his Gospel: Do you know and love Jesus, who is Messiah and Son of God?

The meaning and fullness of life spring from this. Everything else fades into twilight. As Edgar Bruns writes in his essay *The Art and Thought of John*, "The reader is, as it were, blinded by the brilliance of his image and comes away like a man who has looked long at the sun— unable to see anything but its light."

Union with Jesus emerges as John's dominant theme. Through the imagery of the vine and the branches, Christ calls us to inhabit a new space in which we can live without anxiety and fear. "Make your home in me, as I make mine in you" (John 15:4). "Whoever remains in me, with me in him, bears fruit in plenty" (15:5). "As the Father has loved me, so I have loved you. Remain in my love" (15:9).

The poet John Donne cries out for all of us:

> Take me to you, imprison me, for I,
> Except you enthrall me, never shall be free,
> Nor ever chaste, except you ravish me.[10]

Looking at Jesus through the prism of Johannine values offers unique insight into the priorities of discipleship. One's personal relationship with Christ towers over every other consideration. What establishes preeminence in the Christian community is not apostleship or ecclesiastical office, nor titles or territory; not the charismatic gifts of tongues, healing, prophecy, or inspired preaching; but only our response to Jesus' question, "Do you love Me?"

The gospel of John sends a prophetic word to the contemporary church, accustomed to treating charismatic persons with excessive deference: The love of Jesus Christ alone establishes status and confers dignity.

Before Peter was clothed with the mantle of authority, Jesus asked him (not once but three times), "Do you love me?" (John 21:15). The question is not only poignant but also revelatory: "If authority is given, it must be based on love of Jesus."[11]

Leadership in the church is not entrusted to successful fund-raisers, brilliant biblical scholars, administrative geniuses, or spellbinding preachers (though these assets may be helpful), but to those who have been laid waste by a consuming passion for Christ—passionate men and women for whom privilege and power are trivial compared to knowing and loving Jesus. Henri Nouwen elaborates on these qualifications for leadership:

> Christian leaders cannot simply be persons who have well-informed opinions about the burning issues of our time. Their leadership must be rooted in the permanent, intimate relationship with the incarnate Word, Jesus, and they need to find there the source for their words, advice, and guidance.... Dealing with burning issues easily leads to divisiveness because, before we know it, our sense of self is caught up in our opinion about a given subject. But when we are securely rooted in personal intimacy with the source of life, it will be possible to remain flexible but not relativistic, convinced without being rigid, willing to confront without being offensive, gentle and forgiving without being soft, and true witnesses without being manipulative.[12]

We have only to examine the great clefts and fissures in church history, the ragged eras of hatred and strife, to see the disastrous consequences that come when John's criterion for leadership is ignored. We can only shudder at the pain caused by cavalier Christian crusaders across the centuries in the name of orthodoxy.

· · ·

Throughout my retreat with John as my companion and guide, I was struck by his choice of verbs and adverbs in narrating his own perception of Jesus and that of others.

Upon being told by her sister Martha that Jesus had arrived in Bethany and wanted to see her, "Mary got up *quickly* and went to Him" (11:29, emphasis added).

Mary of Magdala is heartbroken and tearful when she finds the tomb empty. At the moment of recognition when Jesus calls her name, she *clung* to him—"Do not cling to me, because I have not yet ascended to the Father" (20:17).

As soon as Peter and John receive word of the empty tomb, they *ran* together to the garden, "but the other disciple, running faster than Peter, reached the tomb first" (20:3-4).

Peter, the denier of Jesus, a failure as a friend in the hour of crisis, a coward in his soul before the servant girl in the courtyard, *jumped* into the water almost naked once John told him Jesus was on shore. "At these words 'It is the Lord,' Simon Peter, who had practically nothing on, wrapped his cloak round him and jumped into the water" (21:7). John notes that the boat was about a hundred yards offshore.

These biblical characters, however clean or tawdry their personal histories may have been, are not paralyzed by the past in their present response to Jesus. Tossing aside self-consciousness, they ran, clung, jumped, and raced to Him. Peter denied Him and deserted Him, but he was not afraid of Him.

Suppose for a moment that in a flash of insight you discovered that all your motives for ministry were essentially egocentric, or suppose that last night you got drunk and committed adultery, or suppose that you failed to respond to a cry for help and the person committed suicide. What would you do?

Would guilt, self-condemnation, and self-hatred consume you, or would you jump into the water and swim a hundred yards at breakneck speed toward Jesus? Haunted by feelings of unworthiness, would you allow the darkness to overcome you, or would you let Jesus be who He is—a Savior of boundless compassion and infinite patience, a Lover who keeps no score of our wrongs?

John seems to be saying that the disciples of Jesus ran to Him because they were crazy about Him; or, in the more restrained prose of Raymond Brown, "Jesus was remembered as one who exhibited love in what he did and was loved deeply by those who followed him."[13]

The beloved disciple sends a message both to the sinner covered with shame and to the local church, tentative and slow to forgive for fear of appearing lax or liberal. The number of people who have fled the church because it is too patient or compassionate is negligible; the number who have fled because they find it too unforgiving is tragic.

...

When Roslyn and I were courting, I seized every opportunity to visit her in New Orleans. In the spring of 1978, after leading a ten-day retreat in Assisi, Italy, for seventy American and Canadian clergy, I flew back with the group to the Twin Cities, arriving at three a.m.

Weary from jet lag and scheduled to speak the following morning at another conference in San Francisco, the obvious and prudent thing to do was to fly directly to the Bay City. Instead I lingered in Minneapolis until six a.m., caught a flight to New Orleans, and shared a delightful picnic with my beloved on the shores of Lake Pontchartrain before journeying on to San Francisco. I landed at midnight.

The next morning I was bright, alert, and energetic, fired by love's urgent longings. I was in love with love.

The root meaning of infatuation derives from the Latin *in-fatuus*, "to make foolish."[14] Experience tells us that life is not always lived to such a lyrical beat. Excitement and enthusiasm must eventually give way to quiet, thoughtful presence. Infatuation must weather separation, loneliness, conflict, tension, and patches of boredom that challenge its capacity to endure. If it is to survive, the illusory intimacy of the first fascination must mature into authentic intimacy characterized by self-sacrifice as well as appreciation of and communication with the beloved.

Many of us can recall an utterly unpredictable moment in which we were deeply affected by an encounter with Jesus Christ—a peak experience that brought immense consolation and heartfelt joy. We were swept up in wonder and love. Quite simply, we were infatuated with Jesus, in love with love. For me the experience lasted nine years.

Then shortly after ordination, I got shanghaied by success. Applause and acclaim in the ministry muffled the voice of the Beloved. I was in demand. What a giddy feeling to have my person admired and my presence required! As my unconditional availability increased and intimacy with Christ decreased, I rationalized that this was the price to be paid for unstinting service to the kingdom enterprise.

Years later, the fame faded and my popularity waned. When rejection and failure first made their unwelcome appearance, I was spiritually unequipped for the inner devastation. Loneliness and sadness invaded my soul. In search of a mood-altering experience, I unplugged the jug. With my predisposition to alcoholism, I was a raging drunk within eighteen months. I abandoned the treasure and took flight from the simple sacredness of my life.

Finally I went for treatment in Minnesota. As the alcoholic fog lifted, I knew there was only one place to go. I sank down into the center of my soul, grew still, and listened to the Rabbi's heartbeat.

The ensuing years have not been marked by uninterrupted awareness of present risenness; my life has not been an unbroken spiral toward holiness. There have been lapses and relapses, fits of pique and frustration, times of high anxiety and low self-esteem. The good news is that their hang time grows progressively shorter.

What is the purpose of this self-disclosure? For anyone caught up in the oppression of thinking that God works only through saints, it offers a word of encouragement. For those who have fulfilled Jesus' prophetic word to Peter—"Before the cock crows you will have disowned me three times" (John 13:38)—it offers a word of liberation. For those trapped in cynicism, indifference, or despair, it offers a word of hope.

Jesus is the same yesterday, today, and forever (Hebrews 13:8). The way He related to Peter, John, and Mary Magdalene is the way He relates to us. The recovery of passion starts with reappraising the value of the treasure, continues with letting the Great Rabbi hold us against His heart, and comes to fruition in a personal transformation of which we will not even be aware.

Not surprisingly, the impostor shrinks as he discovers that, apart from Christ, his alleged virtues are but brilliant vices.

·8·

Fortitude and Fantasy

ANTHONY DE MELLO IN *The Way to Love* wrote bluntly,

Look at your life and see how you have filled its emptiness with people. As a result they have a stranglehold on you. See how they control your behavior by their approval and disapproval. They hold the power to ease your loneliness with their company, to send your spirits soaring with their praise, to bring you down to the depths with their criticism and rejection. Take a look at yourself spending almost every waking moment of your day placating and pleasing people, whether they are living or dead. You live by their norms, conform to their standards, seek their company, desire their love, dread their ridicule, long for their applause, meekly submit to the guilt they lay upon you; you are terrified to go against the fashion in the way you dress or speak or act or even think. And observe how even when you control them you depend on them and are enslaved by them. People have become so much a part of your being that you cannot even imagine living a life that is unaffected or uncontrolled by them.[1]

In John's gospel, the Jews are said to be incapable of believing because they "look to one another for approval" (5:44). There appears to be a radical incompatibility between human respect and authentic faith in

Christ. The strokes or the scorn of our peers become more important than the approval of Jesus.

As I wrote earlier, the dominant sin in my adult life has been my cowardly refusal to think, feel, act, respond, and live from my authentic self, because of fear of rejection. I don't mean that I do not believe in Jesus anymore. I still believe in Him, but peer pressure has set limits to the boundaries of my faith. Nor do I mean that I do not love Jesus anymore. I still love Him very much, but I sometimes love other things—specifically my glittering image—even more. Any self-imposed limit to my faith and love for Jesus inevitably initiates a betrayal of some kind. I march in lockstep with the intimidated apostles: "All the disciples deserted him and ran away" (Matthew 26:56).

The opinions of others exert a subtle but controlling pressure on the words I speak and the words I stuff; the tyranny of my peers controls the decisions I make and the ones I refuse to make. I am afraid of what others may say. Peter G. van Breeman identified this fear:

> *This fear of ridicule paralyzes more effectively than would a head-on attack or an outspoken harsh criticism. How much good is left undone because of our fear of the opinion of others! We are immobilized by the thought: what will others say? The irony of all this is that the opinions we fear most are not those of people we really respect, yet these same persons influence our lives more than we want to admit. This enervating fear of our peers can create an appalling mediocrity.*[2]

...

When we freely assent to the mystery of our belovedness and accept our core identity as Abba's child, we slowly gain autonomy from controlling relationships. We become inner directed rather than outer determined. The fleeting flashes of pleasure or pain caused by the affirmation or deprivation of others will never entirely disappear, but their power to induce self-betrayal will be diminished.

Passion is not high emotion but a steely determination, fired by love, to stay centered in the awareness of Christ's present risenness, a driven-ness to remain rooted in the truth of who I am, and a readiness to pay the price of fidelity. To *own* my unique self in a world filled with voices contrary to the gospel requires enormous fortitude. In this decade of much empty religious talk and proliferating Bible studies, idle intellec-tual curiosity and pretensions of importance, intelligence without cour-age is bankrupt. The truth of faith has little value when it is not also the life of the heart. Thirteenth-century theologian Anthony of Padua opened every class he taught with the phrase, "Of what value is learning that does not turn to love?"

With biting satire, Søren Kierkegaard mocked the pursuit of biblical and theological knowledge as an end in itself:

> *We artful dodgers act as if we do not understand the New Testament, because we realize full well that we should have to change our way of life drastically. That is why we invented "religious education" and "christian doctrine." Another concordance, another lexicon, a few more commentaries, three other translations, because it is all so difficult to understand. Yes, of course, dear God, all of us—capitalists, officials, ministers, house-owners, beggars, the whole society—we would be lost if it were not for "scholarly doctrine!"*[3]

The one great passion in Jesus' life was His Father. He carried a secret in His heart that made Him great and lonely.[4] The four evangelists do not spare us the brutal details of the losses Jesus suffered for the sake of integrity; the price He paid for fidelity to His passion, His person, and His mission. His own family thought He needed custodial care (Mark 3:21), He was called a glutton and a drunkard (Luke 7:34), the religious leaders suspected a demonic seizure (Mark 3:22), and bystanders called Him some bad names. He was spurned by those He loved, deemed a loser, driven out of town, and killed as a criminal.

The pressures of religious conformity and political correctness in our culture bring us face-to-face with what Johannes Metz called "the poverty of uniqueness."[5] On the desk in the study where I wrote this book stands a picture of Thomas Merton with this inscription: "If you forget everything else that has been said, I would suggest you remember this for the future: 'From now on, everybody stands on his own two feet.'"

The poverty of uniqueness is the call of Jesus to stand utterly alone when the only alternative is to cut a deal at the price of one's integrity. It is a lonely *yes* to the whispers of our true self, a clinging to our core identity when companionship and community support are withheld. It is a courageous determination to make unpopular decisions that are expressive of the truth of who we are—not of who we think we should be or who someone else wants us to be. It is trusting enough in Jesus to make mistakes and believing enough that His life will still pulse within us. It is the unarticulated, gut-wrenching yielding of our true self to the poverty of our own unique, mysterious personality.

In a word, standing on our own two feet is an often heroic act of love.

In the name of prudence, the terrified impostor would have us betray our identity and our mission, whatever it might be—standing with a friend in the harsh weather of life, solidarity with the oppressed at the cost of ridicule, refusal to be silent in the face of injustice, unswerving loyalty to a spouse, or any lonely call to duty on a wintry night. Other voices clamor, "Don't make waves; say what everyone else is saying and do what they're doing; tailor your conscience to fit this year's fashion. When in Rome, do as the Romans do. You don't want to raise eyebrows and be dismissed as a kook. Settle in and settle down. You'd be overruled anyway."

Metz wrote,

So the argument runs, urging everyone to the average, thoughtless mediocrity that is veiled and protected by the legalities, conventions and flattery of a society that craves endorsement for every activity, yet retreats into public anonymity. Indeed, with such anonymity it will risk everything—and nothing!—except a genuine, open, personal commitment. Yet without paying the price of poverty implied in such commitments, no one will fulfill her or his mission as a human being. For only poverty enables us to find true selfhood.[6]

Anyone who has ever stood up for the truth of human dignity, no matter how disfigured, only to find previously supportive friends holding back, even remonstrating with you for your boldness, feels the loneliness of the poverty of uniqueness. This happens every day to those who choose to suffer for the absolute voice of conscience, even in what seem to be small matters. They find themselves standing alone. I have yet to meet the man or woman who enjoys such responsibility.

The measure of our depth awareness of Christ's present risenness is our capacity to stand up for the truth and sustain the disapproval of significant others. An increasing passion for truth evokes a growing indifference to public opinion and to what people say or think. We can no longer drift with the crowd or echo the opinions of others. The inner voice—*Take courage. It is I. Do not be afraid*—assures that our security rests in having no security. When we stand on our own two feet and claim responsibility for our unique self, we are growing in personal autonomy, fortitude, and freedom from the bondage of human approval.

A tale often told in Irish pubs catches this spirit of liberation. A tourist was exploring some back roads in a remote corner of Ireland. Rather than risk getting lost, he decided to remain in his car and wait for a local inhabitant to arrive. After a considerable length of time, a local man approached on a bicycle. The tourist greeted him warmly and said, "Well, Paddy, am I glad to see you. I want to know which of these roads will take me back into the village."

"How did you know my name is Paddy?" asked the local man.

"Oh, I just guessed it," replied the tourist.

"Well, in that case, you can guess which is the right road!" said the local man as he rode away angrily.[7]

...

In the past twenty years, both psychology and religion have laid strong emphasis on the primacy of *being* over *doing*. We are often reminded by pastor, therapist, and next-door neighbor, "It is not what you *do* that matters; it is who you *are*." There is certainly an element of truth in this statement—who we are in God is of ultimate significance. Who one *is* transcends what one *does* or what one *says* or what descriptive traits and qualities one *has*.[8]

In religious circles, we have reacted sharply against the heresy of works and the pharisaical focus on the endless doing of ritual acts, which is the undoing of authentic religion. We have been cautioned not to identify ourselves with our career or ministry because when change comes through old age, sickness, or retirement, we will feel worthless and useless and without a clue as to who we are. We reject our Christian culture when it seems to equate holiness with doing. We know that the practice of conferring and withholding honors in the local church is often based on dubious accomplishments.

Again, there is undeniable wisdom here. The tendency to construct a self-image based on performing religious acts easily leads to the illusion of self-righteousness. When our sense of self is tied to any particular task—such as serving in a soup kitchen, promoting environmental consciousness, or giving spiritual instruction—we take a functional approach to life; work becomes the central value; we lose touch with the true self and the happy combination of mysterious dignity and pompous dust which we really are.

And yet . . .

While acknowledging the truth contained in the foregoing paragraphs, I want to affirm that what we *do* may be far more decisive and far more expressive of the ultimate truth of who we *are* in Christ than anything else. I'm not suggesting stockpiling righteousness points to earn a seat at the heavenly banquet through vigorous effort. But who we are is elusive, even to the most sophisticated, therapeutic probing of the human psyche.

Faith tells us that we are Abba's beloved children. Faith persuades us of the present risenness of Jesus. But, as Sebastian Moore noted, "In religion there always lurks the fear that we invented the story of God's love."[9] Genuine faith leads to knowing the love of God, to confessing Jesus as Lord, and to being transformed by what we know.

An old woman lay seriously ill in a hospital. Her closest friend read Isaiah 25:6-9 aloud to her. Wanting the comfort and support of faith, the sick woman asked her friend to hold her hand. On the other side of the bed, her husband, who considered himself a deeply religious man and who prided himself for his boldness in having a "Honk if you love Jesus" bumper sticker on his car, reached out to take her other hand. His wife withdrew it, saying with deep sadness, "Herbert, you are not a believer. Your cruelty and callousness throughout the forty years of our marriage tells me that your faith is an illusion."

Suppose you have a keen dislike for the used-car salesman who knowingly sold you a lemon. You learn that he is in the hospital recuperating from a heart attack. You call his wife and assure her of your prayers and then visit the salesman in the hospital and leave a get-well card with a batch of homemade cookies on his nightstand. You still dislike him and disapprove of his shady tactics. When you lay your head on the pillow that night, why should you dwell more on your dislike and disapproval of him than on the fact that you did a stupendous act of kindness that transcended your feelings? In this case, what you *do* matters more than who you *are*.

Simon Tugwell remarked, "What we do can be much more versatile and worthwhile than what goes on behind the scenes of our psychological life. And it may be of greater significance for our being in God, because it may express his true purpose, even while it does not express anything we could clearly call our own purpose."[10]

Someone might protest, "But to visit the salesman in the hospital is false, two-faced, and hypocritical." I submit that it is the triumph of do-ness over is-ness. When Jesus said, "Love your enemies, *do* good to those who hate you" (Luke 6:27, emphasis added), I do not think He meant that we play kissy-face with them.

Substituting theoretical concepts for acts of love keeps life at a safe distance. This is the dark side of putting *being* over *doing*. Is this not the accusation that Jesus leveled against the religious elite of His day?

The Christian commitment is not an abstraction. It is a concrete, visible, courageous, and formidable way of being in the world—forged by daily choices consistent with inner truth. A commitment that is not visible in humble service, suffering discipleship, and creative love is an illusion. Jesus Christ is impatient with illusions, and the world has no interest in abstractions. "Everyone who listens to these words of mine and does not act on them will be like a stupid man who built his house on sand" (Matthew 7:26). If we bypass these words of the Great Rabbi, the spiritual life will be nothing more than *fantasy*.

As Maurice Blondel once said, "The one who talks, especially if he talks to God, can affect a great deal, but the one who acts really means business and has more claim on our attention. If you want to know what a person really believes, don't listen to what he says but watch what he does."[11]

One day Jesus announced that He had not come to call the virtuous but sinners. Then He proceeded to break bread with a notorious public sinner, Zaccheus. Through table fellowship, Jesus acted out His passion for the Father whose indiscriminate love allows His rain to fall on honest and dishonest men alike. The inclusion of sinners in meal sharing is a dramatic expression of the merciful love of the redeeming God.

Jesus reinforced His words with deeds. He was not intimidated by authority figures. He seemed unfazed by the crowds' complaints that He was violating the law by going to a sinner's house. Jesus broke the law of traditions when the love of persons demanded it.

Begrudgingly, the Pharisees were forced to acknowledge Jesus' integrity: "Master, we know you are an honest man, that you are not afraid of anyone, because a man's rank means nothing to you, and that you teach the way of God in all honesty" (Mark 12:14). Although it was a ploy to trap Him, this admission tells us something of the impact Jesus had on His listeners. A life of integrity has prophetic clout even with cynics. Yes, indeed, this Man was truly a Rabbi unlike any other in Palestine. His Word thundered with authority: He was the Great Rabbi because His being and His doing, like His humanity and His divinity, were one.

At another point in His earthly ministry, Jesus said, "The Son of Man came not to be served but to serve" (Matthew 20:28). On the eve of His death, Jesus took off His outer garment, tied a towel around His waist, poured water into a copper basin, and washed the feet of His disciples. *The Jerusalem Bible* notes that the dress and the duty are those of a slave.

French theologian Yves Congar stated, "The revelation of Jesus is not contained in his teaching alone; it is also, and perhaps we ought to say mainly, in what he did. The coming of the Word into our flesh, God's acceptance of the status of servant, the washing of the disciples' feet—all this has the force of revelation and a revelation of God."[12]

A profound mystery: God becomes a slave. This implies very specifically that God wants to be known through servanthood. Such is God's own self-disclosure. Thus, when Jesus describes His return in glory at the end of the world, He says, "Happy those servants whom the master finds awake when he comes. I tell you solemnly, *he will put on an apron, sit them down at a table and wait on them*" (Luke 12:37, emphasis added).

Jesus remains Lord by being a *servant*.

The beloved disciple presents a mind-bending image of God, blowing away all previous conceptions of who the Messiah is and what discipleship is all about. What a scandalous and unprecedented reversal of the world's values! To prefer to be the servant rather than the lord of the household is the path of downward mobility in an upwardly mobile culture. To taunt the idols of prestige, honor, and recognition . . . to refuse to take oneself seriously or to take seriously others who take themselves seriously . . . to dance to the tune of a different drummer, and to freely embrace the servant lifestyle—these are the attitudes that bear the stamp of authentic discipleship.

The stark realism of John's portrait of Christ leaves no room for romanticized idealism or sloppy sentimentality. Servanthood is not an emotion or mood or feeling; it is a decision to live like Jesus. It has nothing to do with what we feel; it has everything to do with what we *do*—humble service. To listen obediently to Jesus—"If I, then, the Lord and Master, have washed your feet, you should wash each other's feet" (John 13:14)—is to hear the heartbeat of the Rabbi John knew and loved.

When being is divorced from doing, pious thoughts become an adequate substitute for washing dirty feet. The call to the servant lifestyle is both a warning not to be seduced by the secular standard of human greatness and also a summons to courageous faith. As we participate in the foot-washing experience, Jesus addresses us directly, commanding our complete attention as He looks into our eyes and makes this colossal claim: "If you want to know what God is like, look at Me. If you want to learn that your God does not come to rule but serve, watch Me. If you want assurance that you did not invent the story of God's love, listen to My heartbeat."

This staggering and implacable assertion about Himself remains the central notion with which we must come to grips.[13] No one can speak for us. The seriousness of the implications in the confession "Jesus is Lord" reveals the cost of discipleship, the towering significance of trust, and the irreplaceable importance of fortitude. Jesus knew these things, too. Our faith in the Incarnation—the enormous mystery of God drawing aside the curtain of eternity and stepping into human history in the man Jesus—is fantasy if we cling to any image of divinity other than the Servant bowed low in the upper room.

When I get sprayed by the storms of life and find my faith has faltered, my courage has gone south, I often turn to Matthew 14:22-33. Jesus sees the disciples caught up in a squall. It is between three and six a.m. He comes walking toward them on the water. They are terrified. "It is a ghost," they cry out in fear. He says, "Courage! It is I! Do not be afraid."

Peter, nothing if not brash, decides to test the voice. "Lord, if it is you, tell me to come to you across the water." The tentative faith of that fearful "if" quickly deteriorates into sheer terror as Peter begins to walk to Jesus. I find comfort (perhaps perverse pleasure) in knowing that the rock on which Jesus would build the church sank like a stone.

...

The dystopian days in which we live are ripe for panic, as the messianic bean counters have joined forces with the apocalyptic spin doctors to predict the imminent end of the world. They put their personal spin on horrific events such as ethnic cleansing in Iraq, the earthquake in Haiti, and grand-scale terrorism in the United States and abroad. They try to match symbols from the book of Revelation with specific historical events, then prophesy that the global village is teetering on the edge and very soon things will be over for the human adventure.

The bean counters and the spin doctors may be correct in their dire ultimatum—that human history has come to an end and the extermination of the species is at hand. The evils of the present generation may indeed be interpreted as definitive signs of God's final intervention to bring about a fiery climax in awesome destruction and incredible triumph. On the other hand, since Jesus Himself disclaimed any knowledge of the day and the hour (Matthew 24:36), they may be completely mistaken.

The Apocalypse holds a certain morbid fascination for the human mind. It easily outlives the circumstances that give it birth. We always see groups who predict the end of the world over the graves of all former predictions. Symbols are always vulnerable to overliteral minds, and the inflated apocalyptic images seem more prone than most to be taken literally. But the tendency to take it too seriously is due to a disease of the human mind rather than to any inherent fault in the Apocalypse itself.

False prophets, playing on people's innate fear of displeasing God, will abound in the coming years, leading people on wild pilgrimages and creating panic. As we listen to the heartbeat of the Rabbi, we will hear a word of reassurance: "I've told you all this beforehand. Shh! Be still. I am here. All is well."

In place of end-times agitation and thoughts of doom, Jesus tells us to be alert and watchful. We are to avoid the doomsayer and the talk-show crank when they conduct their solemn televised meeting in the green room of the Apocalypse. We are to act justly, to love tenderly, and to walk humbly with our God (Micah 6:8). We are to claim our beloved-ness each day and live as servants in the awareness of present risenness. We pay no heed to the quacks and self-proclaimed seers who manipulate the loyalty of others for their self-serving purposes.

Edward Schillebeeckx, winner of the Erasmus prize as Europe's outstanding theologian, said,

The only correct and adequate answer to the question which was put on all sides in Jesus' time and which in the New Testament the disciples had also put to Jesus—"Lord, when is the end coming, and what are the signs of it?"—is therefore: do not puzzle over such things, but live an ordinary life as Christians, in accordance with the practice of the kingdom of God; then no one and nothing can come upon you unexpectedly apart from the liberating rule of God himself. . . . It does not matter whether you are now working in the field or grinding corn, whether you are a priest or a professor, a cook or a porter, or just an old age pensioner. What matters is how your life looks when you hold it up to the light of the gospel of the God whose nature is to love of all humankind.[14]

...

The movie *The Player*, directed by Robert Altman, offers a chilling portrait of a world that canonizes greed, the deal, the sure thing. The film, satirizing filmmaking itself, condones irresponsible wealth and power, shows contempt for unprofitable originality, and sanctifies self-interest: The bottom line is the only line. Altman implies that Hollywood is a microcosm of us all—a society marinating in its own incestuous self-interest.

One imponderable trait of the human psyche is its ability to make irrational judgments about worthwhile human investments along with its refusal to view life in light of eternity. Whether it be the grandiosity of the addict, the self-importance of the workaholic, the self-interest of the movie mogul, or the self-absorption of the average person in his or her plans and projects—all collaborate to weave the fantasy of invincibility, or what Ernest Becker calls "the denial of death."

Of all the books written and all the sermons preached about death, none has come from firsthand experience. Yes, not one of us has intellectual doubts about death's inevitability. The mute testimony of our ancestors tells us that to deny that death will one day come is literally *fantastic*. Nevertheless, among believers profound consciousness of death is a rarity. For some, the veil between present reality and eternity is the shroud of science—death is simply the last disease waiting to be conquered by medicine. For others, their view is represented by a physician in a respected medical journal: "In my opinion death is an insult; the stupidest, ugliest thing that can ever happen to a human being,"[15] and therefore, a cruel, unwanted interruption that is best ignored. For many the separation from loved ones is too painful to

consider. Perhaps for most of us, the frenetic pace of life and the immediate claims of the present moment leave no time, except for fleeting
reflection at funerals, to contemplate seriously where we came from
and where we are going.

Saint Benedict, the founder of Western monasticism, offers the
sober advice to "keep your own death before your eyes each day." It is
not a counsel to morbidity but a challenge to faith and fortitude. Until
we come to terms with this primal fact of life, as Parker Palmer noted,
there can be no spirituality worth speaking of.

I waffle back and forth between fear and anticipation of death.
I am most afraid of death when I am most afraid of life. When I'm
conscious of my belovedness and when I am alert to the present risenness of Jesus, I can face death courageously. Paul's boast that life,
of course, means Christ, and death is a prize to be won (Philippians
1:21), becomes my own. Without fear I can acknowledge that the
authentic Christian tension is not between life and death, but between
life and life. I buoyantly affirm the Great Rabbi's words on the eve of
His death: "I live and you will live" (John 14:19). Above all, when
He holds me silently against His heart, I can even accept the terror of
abandonment.

But when the night is darkest and the impostor is running amok,
and I am thinking how well I have done and how necessary I am and
how secure I feel in the affirmation of others, and how remarkable
that I've become a player in the religion thing and how deserving I
am of an exotic vacation and how proud my family is of me and how
glorious the future looks—suddenly, like mist rising from the fields,
I am enveloped in thoughts of death. Then I am afraid. I know that
behind all my Christian slogans and conversations about resurrection,
there lurks a very frightened man. Entranced in my reverie, I am isolated and alone. I have joined the cast of Robert Altman's players. Like
a runaway inmate from the asylum, I have escaped into the fantasy
of invincibility.

...

Suppose an eminent physician, well informed of your medical history, told you that you have twenty-four hours to live. You sought a second opinion, which confirmed the first. And a third agreed with the previous two.

When we hear the footsteps of the Grim Reaper, our perception of reality changes drastically. With precious time slipping away like sand in an hourglass, we quickly dismiss all that is petty and irrelevant and focus only on matters of ultimate concern. As Samuel Johnson once said, "The prospect of being hanged concentrates a man's mind wonderfully." Although a panic attack might be our initial response, we soon realize that sobbing is only wasting valuable time.

In one of her novels, Iris Murdoch depicts a man in a boundary situation. Time is running out for him. He is trapped in a cave waist deep in water. Soon the high tide will inundate the place. He thinks, *If I ever get out of here, I will be no man's judge . . . not to judge, not to be superior, not to exercise power, not to seek, seek, seek. To love and to reconcile and to forgive, only this matters. All power is sin and all law is frailty. Love is the only justice. Forgiveness, reconciliation—not law.*[16]

The denial of death is not a healthy option for a disciple of Jesus. Nor is pessimism in the face of today's troubles. The significant shift in priorities that comes through living twenty-four hours at a time is not mere resignation to what we know cannot be changed. My life in the confrontation with trials and tribulations is not stoic passivity. My death-defying *no* to despair at the end of my life and my life-affirming *yes* to seemingly insurmountable problems in the midst of my life are both animated by hope in the invincible might of the risen Jesus and in the *immeasurable scope of His power in us who believe* (Ephesians 1:19).

We are not cowed into timidity by death and life. Were we forced to rely on our own shabby resources, we would be pitiful people indeed. But the awareness of Christ's present risenness persuades us that we are buoyed up and carried on by a life greater than our own. Hope means that in Christ, by entrusting ourselves to Him, we can courageously face evil by accepting our own need for further conversion, the lovelessness of others, and the whole legacy of sin in the world around us and in our own heritage. We can then face death just as we can face life and the mammoth task before us, which Paul described as killing "everything in you that belongs only to earthly life" (Colossians 3:5).

The Christ within who is our hope of glory is not a matter of theological debate or philosophical speculation. He is not a hobby, a part-time project, a good theme for a book, or a last resort when all human effort fails. He is our life, the most real fact about us. He is the power and wisdom of God dwelling within us.

William Johnston was a wise old contemplative teacher at Sophia University in Tokyo. In a letter to a young colleague who was about to open a prayer center, he fairly shouted, "Never banish the thought of death from your consciousness."[17] To those brave souls who long to forego fantasy for a life of fortitude, I would add, "Never deliberately banish the awareness of present risenness, and as you finish reading this chapter, for a moment listen to the Rabbi's heartbeat."

·9·

The Rabbi's Heartbeat

GOD IS LOVE.

Jesus is God.

If Jesus ceased loving, He would cease being God.

Much of contemporary writing on spirituality has elucidated this theme with great clarity and depth. The unconditional love of God is the *leitmotif* of innumerable books, articles, sermons, and conferences. References to a limitless love that knows no boundary, caution, or breaking point are not in short supply either on the Christian analyst's couch, the preacher's pulpit, the theologian's classroom, or Andrew Greeley's novels. To cite a few examples,

The love of God is not a mild benevolence but a consuming fire.

— BEDE GRIFFITHS

God's love is not conditional. We cannot do anything to deserve God's love—for which reason it is called grace; and we need not do anything to provoke it. It is always already there. Any love that is going to be salvific must be of this type, absolutely unconditional and free.

— BEATRICE BRUTEAU, *RADICAL OPTIMISM*

One of the keys to real religious experience is the shattering realization that no matter how hateful we are to ourselves, we are not hateful to God. This realization helps us to understand the difference between our love and His. Our love is a need, His a gift.

— THOMAS MERTON, *THE NEW MAN*

A false and illusory notion of God . . . sees God as someone who is gracious to me when I am good, but who punishes me relentlessly when I am bad. This is a typical patriarchal notion of God. He is the God of Noah who sees people deep in sin, repents that He made them and resolves to destroy them. He is the God of the desert who sends snakes to bite his people because they murmured against Him. He is the God of David who practically decimates a people, because their king, motivated by pride perhaps, takes up a census of his empire. He is the God who exacts the last drop of blood from his Son, so that his just anger, evoked by sin, may be appeased. This God whose moods alternate between graciousness and fierce anger, a god who is still all too familiar to many Christians—is a caricature of the true God. This God does not exist. This is not the God whom Jesus reveals to us. This is not the God whom Jesus called "Abba."

— WILLIAM SHANNON

Those luminous extrapolations of the gospel faithfully echo the words of the Great Rabbi in John's gospel:

- "A man can have no greater love than to lay down his life for his friends." (15:13)
- "I do not say that I shall pray to the Father for you, because the Father himself loves you." (16:26-27)
- "I will not leave you orphans." (14:18)
- "Anybody who loves me will be loved by my Father, and I shall love him and show myself to him." (14:21)
- "I shall see you again, and your hearts will be full of joy." (16:22)

Our response to these wondrous revelations varies widely. One person hears the words, "God loves you as you are and not as you should be," and says, "That is dangerous teaching. It promotes complacency and leads to moral laziness and spiritual laxity." A second responds, "Yes, God loves me as I am, but He loves me so much He won't let me stay where I am."

A third way to respond is from the detached vantage point of the religious dabbler, who reacts to Jesus' self-disclosure with, "Very interesting." Eugene Peterson has a sharp response to this mind-set: "Scripture . . . is not for entertainment. It is not for diversion. It is not for culture. It is not a key for unlocking secrets to the future. It is not a riddle to intrigue the pious dilettante."[1]

A fourth response is the cynical one: "It's all just words, words, words—*abracadabra*." Cynics debunk everything. There is nothing true, good, or beautiful under the sun. In actuality, the cynic is a hurt sentimentalist turned inside out. There is no Santa Claus. "I'll never trust anyone again." "I didn't know what love was until I got married; then it was too late." A father, alienated from his three sons for many years, was asked how he liked children. Quoting W. C. Fields, he replied, "Fried!"

In sexual love the cynic perceives lust; in sacrifice and dedication, guilt; in charity, condescension; in political skills, manipulation; in the powers of the mind, rationalization; in peacefulness, ennui; in neighborliness, self-interest; in friendship, opportunism. The vitality of the old is pathetic; the exuberance of the young is immature; the steadiness of the middle-aged is boredom.[2]

And yet even for the most disillusioned cynic, an aching longing remains for something true, good, or beautiful.

Lastly, we come to the sincere disciples who listen attentively to the Word of God, yet remain curiously unmoved. The words inform them about God but do not involve them in *knowing* God. They respond, "The thoughts and words are beautiful and inspiring." But the problem is, they stop there. Endless rational analysis substitutes for decisive commitment.

The words engage their minds, but their disengaged hearts remain elsewhere and otherwise. They live in a world of what Professor H. H. Price called "uncashed symbols."[3]

The engaged mind, illuminated by truth, awakens awareness; the engaged heart, affected by love, awakens passion. May I say once more—this essential energy of the soul is not an ecstatic trance, a high emotion, or a sanguine stance toward life: It is a fierce longing for God, an unyielding resolve to live in and out of the truth of our belovedness.

The love of Christ (not our love for Him but His love for us) impels us. The integration of mind and heart shapes a unified personality living in a state of *passionate awareness*.

. . .

The unaffected heart is one of the dark mysteries of human existence. It beats dispassionately in human beings with lazy minds, listless attitudes, unused talents, and buried hopes. Like Ian Bedloe's mother, they never seem to get beneath the surface of their lives. They die before they ever learn to live.

Years wasted in vain regrets, energies dissipated in haphazard relationships and projects, emotions blunted—passive before whatever experiences the day brings—they are like snoring sleepers who resent having their peace disturbed. Their existential mistrust of God, the world, and even themselves underlies their inability to make a passionate commitment to anyone or anything.

Paradoxically, we attain self-awareness, not by self-analysis, but by the leap of commitment. According to Viktor Frankl, a person finds identity only to the extent that "he commits himself to something beyond himself, to a cause greater than himself."[4] The meaning of our lives emerges in the surrender of ourselves to an adventure of becoming who we are not yet.

The unaffected heart leaves a legacy of Disney World paraphernalia and a thousand lost golf balls. The sheer vacuity of the unlived life guarantees the person will never be missed. "These people, living on borrowed emotions, stumbling through the corridors of time like shipboard drunks ... never taste life deeply enough to be either saints or sinners."[5]

...

Sebastian Moore made this astonishing confession: "It has taken me thirty years to understand that the admission and forgiveness of sin is the essence of the New Testament."

Before assigning him to a slow learners' group, let us examine carefully our own comprehension of sin and forgiveness. To what extent are we truly reconciled to God and ourselves, and to what degree do we actually dare to live each day as forgiven men and women?

For most of us, the generic confession of sinfulness comes easily—that is, all human beings are sinners; I am human; therefore, I am a sinner. A hasty examination of conscience reveals minor infractions of the law, or what Roman Catholic locution calls "venial sins." This vague admission of wrongdoing is necessary in order to qualify for membership in the community of the saved. But saved from what?

Our blindness to the sinfulness of the late Mother Teresa exposes our superficial understanding of the mystery of iniquity lurking within every human being. Her heroic works of charity shield us from the truth of her inner poverty as well as from our own. For if we emulate her sacrificial love in some small fashion, we are lulled into a false sense of security that persuades us that we have no need of repentance today. When the little Albanian saint humbly confessed her brokenness and her desperate need for God, we are either uncomprehending or we secretly suspect her of false modesty.

Paul Claudel once stated that the greatest sin is to lose the sense of sin. If sin is merely an aberration caused by oppressive social structures, circumstances, environment, temperament, compulsions, and upbringing, we will admit the sinful human condition but deny that we are sinners. We see ourselves as basically nice, benevolent people with minor hang-ups and neuroses that are the common lot of humanity. We rationalize and minimize our terrifying capacity to make peace with evil and thereby reject all that is not nice about us.

The essence of sin lies in the enormity of our self-centeredness, which denies our radical contingency and displaces the sovereignty of God with what Alan Jones calls "our sucking two-percent self." Our fascination with power, prestige, and possessions justifies aggressive self-assertion, regardless of the damage inflicted on others. The impostor insists that looking out for Numero Uno is the only sensible posture in a dog-eat-dog world. "That unwed mother made her own bed," shouts the false self. "Let her lie in it!"

The evil operative within us resides in relentless self-absorption, in what Moore calls "our inescapable narcissism of consciousness."[6] Therein lies the source of our cruelty, possessiveness, jealousy, and every species of malice. If we gloss over our selfishness and rationalize the evil within us, we can only pretend we are sinners and therefore only pretend we have been forgiven. A sham spirituality of pseudorepentance and pseudobliss eventually fashions what modern psychiatry calls a borderline personality, in which appearances make up for reality.

Those who stop short of evil in themselves will never know what love is about.[7] Unless and until we face our sanctimonious viciousness, we cannot grasp the meaning of the reconciliation Christ affected on Calvary's hill.

Humility, recovering alcoholics like to say, is stark, raving honesty. Recovery from the disease cannot be initiated until the deadly denial dwelling in the subterranean personality of the drunk is exposed and acknowledged. He or she must hit bottom, arrive at the moment of truth when the pain it takes to hang on to the bottle becomes much greater than the pain it takes to let go. Similarly, we cannot receive what the crucified Rabbi has to give unless we admit our plight and stretch out our hands until our arms ache.

...

If we search for one word to describe the mission and ministry of Jesus Christ, *reconciliation* would not be a bad choice. "In other words, God in Christ was reconciling the world to himself, not holding men's faults against them" (2 Corinthians 5:19). When Jesus said that if He be lifted up from the earth, He would draw all men and women to Himself, He is referring to His being lifted up on a crossbeam. The body of a help-less Rabbi writhing in agony and bleeding to death is the total and final reversal of our flight from ourselves. Calvary is the unbearable place where all the evil in our shabby selves tries to hold its own against God, "and thus provokes the thunder of resurrection."[8]

Through His *passion* and death Jesus carried away the essential sick-ness of the human heart and broke forever the deadly grip of hypocrisy on our souls. He has robbed our loneliness of its fatal power by traveling Himself to the far reaches of loneliness ("My God, my God, why have You deserted Me?"—Matthew 27:46). He has understood our igno-rance, weakness, and foolishness and granted pardon to us all ("Father, forgive them; they do not know what they are doing"—Luke 23:34). He has made His pierced heart a safe place for every defeated cynic, hope-less sinner, and self-loathing derelict across the bands of time. God rec-onciled *all* things, "everything in heaven and *everything* on earth, when he made peace by his death on the cross" (Colossians 1:20, emphasis added).

The Cross reveals that Jesus has conquered sin and death and that nothing, *absolutely nothing,* can separate us from the love of Christ. Neither the impostor nor the pharisee; neither the lack of awareness nor the lack of passion; neither the negative judgments of others nor the debased perceptions of ourselves; neither our scandalous pasts nor our uncertain futures; neither the power struggles in the church nor the tensions in our marriages; nor fear, guilt, shame, and self-hatred; not even death can tear us away from the love of God, made visible in Jesus the Lord.

Listening to the faint heartbeat of the dying Rabbi is a powerful stimulus to the recovery of passion. It is a sound like no other.

The Crucified says, "Confess your sin so that I may reveal Myself to you as lover, teacher, and friend, that fear may depart and your heart can stir once again with passion." His word is addressed both to those filled with a sense of self-importance and to those crushed with a sense of self-worthlessness. Both are preoccupied with themselves. Both claim a godlike status, because their full attention is riveted either on their prominence or their insignificance. They are isolated and alienated in their self-absorption.

The release from chronic egocentricity starts with letting Christ love them where they are. Consider John Cobb's words:

The spiritual man can love only . . . when he knows himself already loved in his self-preoccupation. Only if man finds that he is already accepted in his sin and sickness, can he accept his own self-preoccupation as it is; and only then can his psychic economy be opened toward others, to accept them as they are—not in order to save himself, but because he doesn't need to save himself. We love only because we are first loved.[9]

· · ·

Julian of Norwich made the startling statement, "Sin will be no shame, but honor." The lives of King David, Peter, Mary Magdalene, and Paul, along with contemporary witnesses such as Etty Hillesum and Charles Colson, lend support to Julian's paradoxical statement. They all faced their capacity for evil, harnessed the power, and by grace converted it into a force for something constructive, noble, and good. This mysterious grace is the active expression of the crucified Christ who has reconciled *all* things in Himself, transforming even our evil impulses into part of the good.

When Jesus told us to love our enemies, He knew that His love operating in us could melt the hardened heart and make the enemy our friend. "This applies supremely," H. A. Williams writes, "to the enemy within. For our own worst enemy is always ourselves. And if with patience and compassion I can love that murderous man, that cruel, callous man, that possessive, envious, jealous man, that malicious man who hates his fellows, that man who is me, then I am on the way to converting him into everything that is dynamically good and lovely and generous and kind and, above all, superabundantly alive with a life which is contagious."[10]

As the angel who troubled the waters said to the physician, "Without your wound where would your power be?"

A man in Australia decided that life was too hard for him to bear. However, he ruled out suicide. Instead, he bought a large corrugated iron tank and furnished it simply with the necessities of life. He hung a crucifix on the wall to remind him of the Rabbi and to help him pray. There he lived a blameless, solitary life, but with one great hardship.

Every morning and evening volleys of bullets would rip through the walls of his tank. He learned to lie on the floor to avoid being shot. Still the bullets ricocheted off the corrugated iron, and the man sustained several wounds. The walls were pierced with many holes that let in the wind and the daylight and some water when the weather was wet. As he plugged up the holes, he cursed the unknown marksman. When he appealed to the police, they were not helpful, and there was little he could do on his own about the situation.

Slowly he began to use the bullet holes for positive purposes. He would gaze out through one hole or another and watch the people passing by, the children flying kites, lovers walking hand in hand, the clouds in the sky, the flight of birds, flowers in bloom, the rising of the moon. In observing these things he would forget himself.

The day came when the tank rusted and finally fell to pieces. He walked out of it with little regret. There was a man with a rifle standing outside.

"I suppose you will kill me now," said the man who had come out of the tank. "But before you do, I would like to know one thing. Why have you been persecuting me? Why are you my enemy, when I have never done you any harm?"

The other man laid the rifle down and smiled at him. "I am not your enemy," he said. And the man who had come out of the tank saw that there were scars on the other man's hands and feet, and these scars were shining like the sun.[11]

The lives of those fully engaged in the human struggle will be riddled with bullet holes. Whatever happened in the life of Jesus is in some way going to happen to us. Wounds are necessary. The soul has to be wounded as well as the body. To think that the natural and proper state is to be without wounds is an illusion.[12] Those who wear bulletproof vests protecting themselves from failure, shipwreck, and heartbreak will never know what love is. The unwounded life bears no resemblance to the Rabbi.

Shortly after I entered seminary, I went to a priest and told him about innumerable bouts of heavy drinking during my three years in the Marine Corps and how I grieved over time squandered in self-indulgence. To my surprise he smiled and said, "Rejoice and be glad. You will have a heart of compassion for those who walk that lonely road. God will use your brokenness to bless many people." As Julian of Norwich said, "Sin will be no shame, but honor." The dualism between good and evil is overcome by the crucified Rabbi who has reconciled all things in Himself. We need not be eaten alive by guilt. We can stop lying to ourselves. The reconciled heart says that everything that has happened to me had to happen to make me who I am—*without exception.*

Thomas Moore adds this insight: "Our depressions, jealousies, narcissism, and failures are not at odds with the spiritual life. Indeed, they are essential to it. When tended, they prevent the spirit from zooming off into the ozone of perfectionism and spiritual pride."[13]

Does this gentle approach lead to self-complacency? One who has listened to the heartbeat of the disgraced Rabbi, spurned and avoided by men and wounded by our transgressions, would never ask such a question.

...

Only in a relationship of the deepest intimacy can we allow another person to know us as we truly are. It is difficult enough for us to live with the awareness of our stinginess and shallowness, our anxieties and infidelities, but to disclose our dark secrets to another is intolerably risky. The impostor does not want to come out of hiding. He will grab for the cosmetic kit and put on his pretty face to make himself "presentable."

Whom can I level with? To whom can I bare my soul? Whom dare I tell that I am benevolent and malevolent; chaste and randy; compassionate and vindictive; selfless and selfish; that beneath my brave words lives a frightened child; that I dabble in religion and in pornography; that I have blackened a friend's character, betrayed a trust, violated a confidence; that I am tolerant and thoughtful, a bigot and a blowhard, and that I really hate okra?

The greatest fear of all is that if I expose the impostor and lay bare my true self, I will be abandoned by my friends and ridiculed by my enemies.

Lately, my attention has been snagged by one verse in Isaiah: "Your salvation lay in conversion and tranquility, *your strength, in complete trust*" (30:15, emphasis added). Our obsession with privacy is rooted in the fear of rejection. If we sense nonacceptance, we cannot lay down the burden of sin; we can only shift the heavy suitcase from one hand to the other. Likewise, we can only lay bare our sinful hearts when we are certain of receiving forgiveness.

I cannot admit that I have done wrong; I cannot admit that I have made a huge mistake, except to someone whom I know accepts me. The person who cannot admit that he is wrong is desperately insecure. At root he does not feel accepted, and so he represses his guilt; he covers his tracks. And so we get the paradox: Confession of fault requires a good self-concept. Repression of fault means a bad self-concept.[14]

Our salvation and our strength lie in complete trust in the Great Rabbi who broke bread with the outcast Zacchaeus. His meal sharing with a notorious sinner was not merely a gesture of liberal tolerance and humanitarian sentiment. It embodied His mission and His message offering forgiveness, peace, and reconciliation to all, without exception.

Again, the answer to the question "Who am I?" comes not from self-analysis but through personal commitment. The heart converted from mistrust to trust in the irreversible forgiveness of Jesus Christ is nothing less than a new creation, and all ambiguity about personal identity is blown away. So awesome is this supreme act of confidence in the Rabbi's acceptance that one can only stutter and stammer about its protean, monumental importance. It is the landmark decision of life, outside of which nothing has value and inside of which every relationship and achievement, every success and failure, derives its meaning. It deals a mortal blow to cynicism, self-hatred, and despair. It is a decisive "I do" to the Rabbi's call, "Trust in God still, and trust in me" (John 14:1). Sebastian Moore wrote,

> *The gospel confession of sin is the most generous, secure, adventurous expression of the human heart. It is the risk that is only taken in the certainty of being acceptable and accepted. It is the full and final expression of that confidence. Only to your lover do you expose your worst. To an amazed world Jesus presents a God who calls for this confession only so that he may reveal himself in a person's depths as his lover. This confession in a context of divine acceptance releases the deepest energies of the human spirit and constitutes the gospel revolution in its essence.*[15]

The promised peace that the world cannot give is located in being in right relationship with God. Self-acceptance becomes possible only through the radical trust in Jesus' acceptance of me as I am. Befriending the impostor and the pharisee within marks the beginning of reconciliation with myself and the end of spiritual schizophrenia.

In the Rabbi's embrace, our evil impulses are converted and transformed into good. Just as the unbridled lust of the sinful woman in Luke's gospel was transformed into a passion for intimacy with Jesus, so our possessiveness about money metastasizes into greed for the treasure in the field. Our inner murderer becomes capable of murdering homophobia, bigotry, and prejudice. Our vindictiveness and hatred are transformed into intolerance and rage at the caricatures of God as a petty accountant. Our chronic niceness is converted into heartfelt compassion for those who have lost their way.

And the meaning of the Rabbi's words, "Behold, I am making *all* things new" (Revelation 21:5, NASB—emphasis added), becomes luminously clear.

...

From among the many messianic titles conferred on Jesus, some used by His contemporaries, others bestowed by the early church— Lord, Master, Savior, Redeemer, King, Pantocrator, Messiah—I have focused on *Rabbi* for two reasons.

First, as I retrace the steps down the cobbled road of my life, I remember the quality of my days before I encountered Christ. I vividly recall the emptiness I felt as I drifted aimlessly from one relationship to another, one tavern to another, seeking solace from the loneliness and boredom of my desiccated heart.

Suddenly Jesus appeared out of nowhere, and life began anew. From being a nobody who cared about nothing but my own comfort, I became somebody, a beloved disciple, who cared about people and things. His

Word became "a light on my path" (Psalm 119:105). I found a sense of direction and purpose, a reason for bounding out of bed in the morning. Jesus was my Rabbi, my Teacher. With infinite patience He illuminated the meaning of life and refreshed the weariness of my defeated days. I cannot and will not forget the Great Rabbi who led me out of darkness into daylight. He is not a refuge from reality but the Way into its depths.

Second, the title *Rabbi* reminds us of the essential Jewishness of Jesus and of our own Semitic origins. Abraham is our father in faith. In the realm of spirit, we are all Semites. As Paul wrote, the Jews "were adopted as sons, they were given the glory and the covenants; the Law and the ritual were drawn up for them, and the promises were made to them. They are descended from the patriarchs and from their flesh and blood came Christ who is above all" (Romans 9:4-5).

Amid the current rise of anti-Semitism around the world, I want never to forget the special status of our Jewish kinfolk. Anti-Semitism is spit on the face of our Jewish Savior. To our shame, much of it is Christian spit.

A Jew of our own generation wrote gently but firmly, "We [Jews] must . . . question, in the light of the Bible, whether the message of the Old Testament which the New Testament claims has been fulfilled, has in fact been fulfilled in history, in the history lived and suffered by us and our ancestors. And here, my dear Christian readers, we must give a negative reply. We can see no kingdom and no peace and no redemption."[16]

The tear-stained face of the Rabbi is ever before my eyes as I contemplate our past unchristian behavior toward our Jewish brothers and sisters. As Burghardt suggests, we need a fresh theology of Judaism and its destiny. We need more dialogue, more interfaith worship and communion. We need to meditate on the words of Shylock in Shakespeare's *The Merchant of Venice* (here we can include any group of oppressed people): "Hath not a Jew eyes? Hath not a Jew hands, organs, dimensions, senses, affections, passions? Fed with the same food, hurt with the same weapons, subject to the same diseases, healed by the same means, warmed and cooled by the same winter and summer, as a Christian is? If you prick us, do we not bleed? if you tickle us, do we not laugh? If you poison us, do we not die?"

Calling Jesus *Rabbi* stirs our sensitivity to both His and our solidarity with the sons and daughters of Abraham as well as the sons and daughters of shame.

...

The bride in the Song of Songs says, "I sleep, but my heart is awake. I hear my Beloved knocking. 'Open to me, my sister, my love, my dove, my perfect one. . . . My beloved thrust his hand through the hole in the door; I trembled to the core of my being. Then I rose to open to my Beloved, myrrh ran off my hands, pure myrrh off my fingers, on to the handle of the bolt" (5:2,4-5).

The ragtag cabal of disciples who have caught the spirit of the bride, opened the door to Jesus, reclined at the table, and listened to His heartbeat will experience at least four things.[17]

First, listening to the Rabbi's heartbeat is immediately a Trinitarian experience. The moment you press your ear against His heart, you instantly hear Abba's footsteps in the distance. I do not know how this happens. It just does. It is a simple movement from intellectual cognition to experiential awareness that Jesus and the Father are one in the Holy Spirit, the bond of infinite tenderness between Them. Without reflection or premeditation, the cry "Abba, I belong to You" rises spontaneously from the heart. The awareness of being sons and daughters in the Son dawns deep in our souls, and Jesus' unique passion for the Father catches fire within us. In the Abba experience, we prodigals, no matter how bedraggled, beat up, or burnt out, are overcome by a Paternal fondness of such depth and tenderness that it beggars speech. As our hearts beat in rhythm with the Rabbi's heart, we come to experience a graciousness, a kindness, a compassionate caring that surpasses our understanding. "That is the enigma of the gospel: How can the Transcendent Other be so incredibly near, so unreservedly loving?"[18] We have only one explanation—the Teacher says that is the way He is.

Second, we realize that we are not alone on the Yellow Brick Road. Traffic is heavy. Fellow travelers are everywhere. It isn't just me and Jesus anymore. The road is dotted with the moral and the immoral, the beautiful and the grungy, friends and enemies, people who help us and those who hinder us, bank guards and bank robbers—human beings of bewildering complexity and diversity. And the Rabbi's word, of course, is to love each person along the way. What we do to them, we do to Him.

We have known this all along.

Early on in Sunday school or catechism class, we learned the Golden Rule: "Always treat others as you would like them to treat you" (Matthew 7:12). Yet our melancholy marriages, dysfunctional families, splintered churches, and loveless neighborhoods indicate that we have not learned well.

"Learning by heart" is another matter entirely. The rhythm of relentless tenderness in the Rabbi's heart makes loving terribly personal, terribly immediate, and terribly urgent. He says, "I give you a new commandment; it is My commandment; it is *all* I command you: Love one another as I have loved you." Only compassion and forgiveness count. Love is the key to everything. Living and loving are one.

Heart speaks to heart. The Rabbi implores, "Don't you understand that discipleship is not about being right or being perfect or being efficient? It's all about the way you live with each other." In every encounter we either give life or we drain it. There is no neutral exchange. We enhance human dignity, or we diminish it. The success or failure of a given day is measured by the quality of our interest and compassion toward those around us. We define ourselves by our response to human need. The question is not how we feel about our neighbor but what we have done for him or her. We reveal our heart in the way we listen to a child, speak to the person who delivers mail, bear an injury, and share our resources with the indigent.

An old anecdote is told about a farm boy whose one skill was finding lost donkeys. When asked how he did this, he answered, "I just figured out where I would go if I were a jackass, and there it was." Turning this in a more positive direction, listening to the Rabbi's heartbeat, the disciple hears where Jesus would be in any given situation, and there He is.

Third, when we recline at the table with Jesus, we will learn that the recovery of passion is intimately connected with the discovery of the passion of Jesus.

An extraordinary transaction takes place between Jesus and Peter on the Tiberias shore. The most plaintive words ever spoken take the form of a heart-stopping question: "Do you love Me?" (John 21:15) As we lay aside our fuzzy distractions and actively listen, we hear the suffering cry of a *God never heard of before*. What is going on here? No deity of any world religion has ever condescended to inquire how we feel about that god. The pagan gods fired thunderbolts to remind peons who was in charge. The Rabbi in whom infinity dwells asks if we care about Him. The Jesus who died a bloody, God-forsaken death that we might live, is asking if we love Him!

The etymological root of *passion* is the Latin verb *passere*, "to suffer." The passion of Jesus in His dialogue with Peter is "the voluntary laying oneself open to another and allowing oneself to be intimately *affected by* him; that is to say, the suffering of passionate love."[19]

The vulnerability of God in permitting Himself to be affected by our response, the heartbreak of Jesus as He wept over Jerusalem for not receiving Him, are utterly astounding. Christianity consists primarily not in what we do for God but in what God does for us—the great, wondrous things that God dreamed up and achieved for us in Christ Jesus. When God comes streaming into our lives in the power of His Word, all He asks is that we be stunned and surprised, let our mouths hang open, and begin to breathe deeply.

The recovery of passion is intimately connected with astonishment. We are swept up by the overwhelming force of mystery. Self-consciousness evaporates in the presence of what Rudolf Otto called "mysterium tremendum." The transcendent God overtakes us and overcomes us. Such an experience may wash over our consciousness like a gentle tide saturating the mind and heart in a tranquil spirit of profound adoration. Awe, wonder, and amazement induce speechless humility. We have a brief glimpse of the God we never dreamed existed.

Or we may be hammered by what the Hebrew tradition calls the *kabod Yahweh*—the crushing majesty of God. A deep, chilling stillness invades the inner sanctum of the soul. The awareness dawns that God is totally Other. The gulf between Creator and creature is unbridgeable. We are specks of sand on a beach of infinite expanse. We are in the magisterial presence of God. Stripped of our credentials of independence, our executive swagger disappears. Living in the wisdom of accepted tenderness is no longer adequate. God's name is Mercy.

Faith stirs, and our fear and trembling find their voices once more. In worship we move into the tremendous poverty that is the adoration of God. We have moved from the Upper Room, where John laid his head on the breast of Jesus, to the book of Revelation, where the beloved disciple fell prostrate before the Lamb of God.

Wise men and women have long held that happiness lies in being yourself without inhibitions. Let the Great Rabbi hold you silently against His heart. In learning who He is, you will find out who you are: Abba's child in Christ our Lord.

Internalizing the Book: Guide for Group Study

THERE ARE TWO WAYS TO read a book, and I have used both. The first way is an external reading in order to gather information that I will employ as an aid to write a sermon, to lead a discussion, to quote in a book I am writing, to support my position in a debate, or to determine whether this particular book would be helpful to a seeker or a struggling friend.

The second way is an internal reading in order to experience the content and to personalize the God described within its pages. This approach requires that I read slowly, frequently pause to meditate on the paragraph or page just read, and sometimes read the entire book a second time. I seek transformation more than information, and the time devoted to the task is soaked in prayer.

I have learned through personal experience that sharing insights and reflections with a small group in a prayerful setting is an invaluable help. When circumstances do not allow for such a gathering, the Holy Spirit will not leave you an orphan. In the absence of a small group, I do encourage journaling, as this practice helps you see your own thoughts. Trust me, it helps. You'll notice there is only one question/thought for each chapter. This is intentional; one question, thoroughly wrestled with, is sufficient—maybe even more than sufficient. Thus, I present the following guide for group or individual use.

Chapter One—Come Out of Hiding

Begin with three minutes of silent prayer, becoming aware in faith of the Indwelling Presence and humbly asking the Spirit to speak to your heart through Scripture, personal reflection, and the insights of others.

Let one from the group read aloud Romans 7:14-25. Then focus on the following questions for personal reflection and group interaction.

- We've all experienced personal failure, and chances are good afterward we've all beaten ourselves up with words like *jerk, stupid, hypocrite, loser,* and *I'm so ashamed I'd like to crawl in a hole.* The temptation in those moments is to then project our own feelings onto God, assuming that He feels the same way about us.

    Reflect on an experience when low self-esteem and self-rejection really did a number on your relationship with Jesus. How did you come out of that? Was it a long or short process? How did you handle it the next time an experience like that came along—because it did, didn't it?

Chapter Two—The Impostor

Begin with three minutes of silent prayer, becoming aware in faith of the Indwelling Presence and humbly asking the Spirit to speak to your heart through Scripture, personal reflection, and the insights of others.

Let one from the group read aloud Mark 8:34-36. Then focus on the following questions for personal reflection and group interaction.

- Describe in some detail the two most prominent disguises your impostor has worn in recent years. What manifestation of the false self are you coping with at the present moment? Self-acceptance goes a-begging until the impostor is acknowledged and accepted. What is denied cannot be healed. Have you embraced your false self, introduced him/her to Jesus, and observed the little rascal beginning to shrink? If not, why not? Have you tagged him/her with a nickname? As to that last question, if not, do that today—give him/her a nickname, for in naming the beast you take away some of its power.

Chapter Three—The Beloved

Begin with three minutes of silent prayer, becoming aware in faith of the Indwelling Presence and humbly asking the Spirit to speak to your heart through Scripture, personal reflection, and the insights of others.

Let one from the group read aloud John 17:23, 26. Then focus on the following meditation and questions for personal reflection and group interaction.

- Jesus prayed to Abba thus: "I have made your name known to them and will continue to make it known, so that the love with which you loved me may be in them" (John 17:26) Does it seem outrageous and incredible—even blasphemous—that Abba loves you just as much as He loves Jesus? But that is precisely what this Bible passage says. I love some people more than others; for example, I love Binky 90 percent, Winky 50 percent, and Stinky 20 percent. Abba cannot do that. If we think that Abba measures His love based on our achievements, we are thinking not of Abba but of ourselves. We *have* love. God *is* love. His love is not a dimension of Himself: It is His whole self. Even a vague intuition of this truth allows us to see the impossibility of Abba loving Jesus 100 percent, Mother Teresa 70 percent, and you 10 percent. If He could, Abba would not be God.

  Right now, in this moment, what "percent" do you believe Abba loves you? There's no value in fudging here—be honest. What might it take for you to begin defining yourself radically as Abba's beloved child—100 percent? Are you even sure that's possible? If not, why not?

Chapter Four—Abba's Child

Begin with three minutes of silent prayer, becoming aware in faith of the Indwelling Presence and humbly asking the Spirit to speak to your heart through Scripture, personal reflection, and the insights of others.

Let one from the group read aloud Matthew 12:17-21 and Galatians 5:6. Then focus on the following questions for personal reflection and group interaction.

- The truest test of our faith is how we live with each other day by day. Do I give life to others, or do I drain life from others through my negativity? In my relationships, do I leave a person feeling a little better or a little worse? Am I in the habit of offering to others what they need most for their lives—a word of encouragement? Let each person in the group share one experience of depriving a person and one experience of affirming a person, and then one experience of being deprived and one of being affirmed.

Chapter Five—The Pharisee and the Child

Begin with three minutes of silent prayer, becoming aware in faith of the Indwelling Presence and humbly asking the Spirit to speak to your heart through Scripture, personal reflection, and the insights of others.

Let one from the group read aloud Matthew 18:1-4. Then focus on the following meditation and questions for personal reflection and group interaction.

- How long does a child hold a grudge, nurture a bitter memory, carry resentment, or harbor hatred in his/her heart? One afternoon while jogging, I saw two seven-year-olds get into a fight. Being a true instrument of peace, I ducked into a doorway to watch the outcome. The heavier boy soon mastered the skinny kid, pinned his wrists to the ground, and asked, "Give up?" The vanquished surrendered. A minute later, while dusting off their pants, the victor said, "Wanna piece of my bubble gum?" The vanquished said, "Yeah," and they went off down the street arm in arm.

Trusting that what is said in the group stays in the group, share with complete candor your struggles with resentments, anger, hardheartedness, and unforgiveness. Be as specific as you can— vagueness is not helpful in this exercise. Yes, it is possible this may involve someone in your small group. Now ask the group to pray over you for the grace to forgive yourself and anyone who has wounded you.

Chapter Six—Present Risenness

Begin with three minutes of silent prayer, becoming aware in faith of the Indwelling Presence and humbly asking the Spirit to speak to your heart through Scripture, personal reflection, and the insights of others.

Let one from the group read aloud John 15:1-5. Then focus on the following meditation and questions for personal reflection and group interaction.

• The great Southern writer Eudora Welty once explained the *raison d'etre* of her short stories and novels: "My wish, my continuing passion, would be not to point the finger in judgment but to part a curtain, that invisible shadow that falls between people, the veil of indifference to each other's presence, each other's wonder, each other's human plight." The veil of indifference to the present risenness of Jesus among many Christians is a bewildering mystery. "These people, living on borrowed emotions, stumbling through the corridors of time like shipboard drunks . . . never taste life deeply enough to be either saints or sinners."[1]

Describe from personal experience your daily efforts to stay centered, to overcome busyness and self-absorption in order to remain aware of the risen Christ abiding within you. What does it look like—are there actual physical disciplines you practice? What does it sound like—is there self-talk going on? Do you listen to music? And what does it feel like—is there a sense of gratitude, or duty, or what?

Chapter Seven—The Recovery of Passion

Begin with three minutes of silent prayer, becoming aware in faith of the Indwelling Presence and humbly asking the Spirit to speak to your heart through Scripture, personal reflection, and the insights of others.

Let one from the group read aloud John 13:23-25. Then focus on the following meditation and questions for personal reflection and group interaction.

* The story of the old man who, as he lay dying, rested his head on the empty chair has been preached by pastors in little congregations of sixty members, by a youth pastor to a crowd of teenagers at a music festival at Wembley Stadium in London, and by Bill Hybels to his twenty thousand–plus community in Willow Creek, Illinois; it has been quoted, rewritten, retold, and embellished in tiny hamlets and large cities.

  What stirs within you when you read this story? Does it express the cry in your heart for intimate belonging? Does it embarrass you? Or do you have some other reaction to it? One of the cardinal rules of prayer is this: Pray as you can; don't pray as you can't. Share with the group the kind of praying you are most comfortable with. Remember the only way to fail in prayer is not to show up.

Chapter Eight—Fortitude and Fantasy

Begin with three minutes of silent prayer, becoming aware in faith of the Indwelling Presence and humbly asking the Spirit to speak to your heart through Scripture, personal reflection, and the insights of others.

Let one from the group read aloud Matthew 14:22-23. Since there are a number of themes in this chapter, such as authority and service, the poverty of uniqueness, being and doing, and so forth, the group may decide to ignore the following questions and to focus on issues more immediate and relevant to your life situations.

- Lacking a lively awareness of my core identity as Abba's child, it is relatively easy to become enslaved to the approval and disapproval of others. Jesus reproved the Pharisees for looking to one another for approval. Share with the group the snares and pitfalls you have experienced recently—flattery of peers, people pleasing, name-dropping, manipulation, excessive friendliness—in order to gain the esteem of others.

  Next, give an example or two of the occasions when you refused to be intimidated and spoke the truth in your heart, fully aware that you would incur the wrath or disfavor of significant others. How did it go? As you expected? Different than you expected? How did you feel several days after that courageous moment?

Chapter Nine—The Rabbi's Heartbeat

Begin with three minutes of silent prayer, becoming aware in faith of the Indwelling Presence and humbly asking the Spirit to speak to your heart through Scripture, personal reflection, and the insights of others.

Let one from the group read aloud John 14:23, John 15:4, and 1 Corinthians 6:19. Then focus on the following meditation and questions for personal reflection and group interaction.

- Yo-Yo Ma, acclaimed as the greatest classical cellist of our era, was told by his mentor at age nineteen, "You have not yet found your sound." Yo-Yo (his name in Chinese means "friend") was stunned. His technical genius was unrivaled at the time; it was simply incomprehensible that he still had not found his own unique sound. "It will take at least ten years," said his mentor. Eleven years later, after learning love and generosity through marriage and having children and holding conversations in his mind with dead classical composers, Yo-Yo at last found his sound.

  After reading the manuscript for my fifth book, *A Stranger to Self-Hatred*, my first publisher, Tom Coffey, said, "I believe you have found your voice." After reading this book, share your final reflections. Have you found your sound, your voice, your true self? Has *Abba's Child* reinforced an identity you have already claimed? Do you believe in the depths of your bones that your Abba is very fond of you? Because He is, you know. And how will your awareness of your belovedness affect your relations with family, friends, and strangers? Because He is very fond of them as well.

If you experienced this book with a small group, I suggest concluding your final meeting time with a party. Eat, drink, and be as merry, as is fitting for those whom Abba loves! Why? Children just love parties. And if you experienced this book by yourself, then treat yourself in some special way. I heartily recommend ice cream!

Notes

CHAPTER ONE — COME OUT OF HIDING

1. Flannery O'Connor, *The Collected Works of Flannery O'Connor* (New York: Farrar, Straus & Giroux, 1991), 42–54.
2. Richard J. Foster, *Prayer: Finding the Heart's True Home* (San Francisco, CA: HarperCollins, 1992), 1.
3. Nicholas Harnan, *The Heart's Journey Home: A Quest for Wisdom* (Notre Dame, IN: Ave Maria Press, 1992), 61.
4. Julian of Norwich, *Revelations of Divine Love* (New York: Penguin, 1966), 56.
5. Thomas Merton, *The Hidden Ground of Love: Letters* (New York: Farrar, Straus & Giroux, 1985), 146.
6. Simon Tugwell, *The Beatitudes: Soundings in Christian Tradition* (Springfield, IL: Templegate Publishers, 1980), 130.
7. Thomas Merton, *Contemplative Prayer* (New York: Doubleday Religion, 1969), 48.
8. David Seamands, *Healing for Damaged Emotions* (Wheaton, IL: Victor, 1981), 49.
9. Morton Kelsey, *Encounter with God: A Theology of Christian Experience*, quoted by Parker Palmer in "The Monastic Way to Church Renewal," *Desert Call* (Winter 1987): 8–9.
10. Henri J. M. Nouwen, *Life of the Beloved: Spiritual Living in a Secular World* (New York: Crossroad, 1992), 21.
11. James Finley, *Merton's Palace of Nowhere: A Search for God Through Awareness of the True Self* (Notre Dame, IN: Ave Maria Press, 1978), 53.
12. Julian of Norwich, chapter 73.
13. Thornton Wilder, *The Angel That Troubled the Waters and Other Plays* (New York: Coward-McCann, 1928), 20.
14. Henri J. M. Nouwen, *The Wounded Healer: Ministry in Contemporary Society* (New York: Doubleday, 1972), 34.
15. James A. Knight, M.D., in *Psychiatry and Religion: Overlapping Concerns*, ed. Lillian Robinson, M.D. (Washington, DC: American Psychiatric Press, 1986). Knight's splendid article, "The Religio-Psychological Dimension of Wounded Healers," is the principal source of my reflections here. My gratitude to him and Lillian Robinson for introducing me to the book.
16. Rainer Maria Rilke, *Letters to a Young Poet* (New York: W. W. Norton, 1962), quoted by Knight, 36.
17. Georges Bernanos, *Diary of a Country Priest* (New York: Sheed and Ward, 1936), 178.

CHAPTER TWO — THE IMPOSTOR

1. Walter J. Burghardt, *To Christ I Look: Homilies at Twilight* (New York/Mahwah, NJ: Paulist, 1989), 15. From "Zapping the Zelig" in another collection of his homilies, *Still Proclaiming Your Wonders*. He has mentored me through his books in the effective use of films, novels, poetry, music, and other contemporary American words and symbols in communicating the gospel. The London *Tablet* calls Burghardt "the grand old man of American homilists."

2. James F. Masterson, M.D., *The Search for the Real Self* (New York: Free Press, 1988), 67.

3. John Bradshaw, *Homecoming: Reclaiming and Championing Your Inner Child* (New York/Toronto: Bantam Books, 1990), 8.

4. Susan Howatch, *Glittering Images* (New York: Ballantine Books, 1987), 278.

5. Thomas Merton, quoted by James Finley in *Merton's Palace of Nowhere: A Search for God Through Awareness of the True Self* (Notre Dame, IN: Ave Maria Press, 1978), 34.

6. Howatch, 162.

7. Masterson, 63.

8. Masterson, 66.

9. Masterson, 65.

10. Jeffrey D. Imbach, *The Recovery of Love: Christian Mysticism and the Addictive Society* (New York: Crossroad, 1992), 62–63.

11. James Finley, *Merton's Palace of Nowhere: A Search for God Through Awareness of the True Self* (Notre Dame, IN: Ave Maria Press, 1978), 36.

12. Parker Palmer, "The Monastic Way to Church Renewal," *Desert Call* (Winter 1987): 8–9.

13. Thomas Merton, *New Seeds of Contemplation* (New York: New Directions, 1961), 35.

14. Simon Tugwell, *The Beatitudes: Soundings in Christian Tradition* (Springfield, IL: Templegate Publishers, 1980), 112.

15. Philomena Agudo, *Intimacy*, the third Psychotheological Symposium (Whitinsville, MA: Affirmation Books, 1978), 21.

16. C. G. Jung, *Modern Man in Search of a Soul* (New York: Harcourt, Brace & World Harvest Books, 1933), 235.

CHAPTER THREE — THE BELOVED

1. William Least Heat-Moon, *Blue Highways: A Journey into America* (New York: Fawcett Crest, 1982), 108–109.

2. Monica Furlong, *Merton: A Biography* (San Francisco, CA: Harper & Row, 1980), 18.

3. John Eagan, *A Traveler Toward the Dawn: The Spiritual Journey of John Eagan* (Chicago: Loyola University Press, 1990), xii.

4. Thomas Merton, quoted by James Finley in *Merton's Palace of Nowhere: A Search for God Through Awareness of the True Self* (Notre Dame, IN: Ave Maria Press, 1978), 71.

5. Eagan, 150–151.

6. Henri J. M. Nouwen, *Life of the Beloved: Spiritual Living in a Secular World* (New York: Crossroad, 1992), 26.

7. Finley, 96.

8. Mike Yaconelli, *The Back Door*. A column written by Yaconelli, editor of *The Door*, a bimonthly Christian periodical that was biting, irreverent, satirical, often serious, occasionally sophomoric, frequently hilarious, never dull, frequently provocative, surprisingly spiritual—my favorite, most enjoyable subscription, and as the advertisement says, "the perfect gift for the closed mind."

9. Walker Percy, *The Second Coming* (New York: Farrar, Straus & Giroux, 1980), 124. Two of Percy's novels—*The Moviegoer,* which won the Pulitzer Prize in 1952, and *Lancelot*—explore the search for the true self and use this literary form to examine authentic and bogus Christianity.

10. Edward Schillebeeckx, *The Church and Mankind* (New York: Seabury Press, 1976), 118.

11. Anthony Padovano, an excerpt from "The Ministerial Crisis in Today's Church," his Saturday morning address during the FCM annual convention on August 18, 1984, Chicago, Illinois.

12. Abraham Heschel, *Between God and Man: An Interpretation of Judaism* (New York: Simon & Schuster, 1959), 41.

13. Frederich Buechner, *The Clown in the Belfry: Writings on Faith and Fiction* (San Francisco, CA: HarperSanFrancisco, 1992), 171.

CHAPTER FOUR — ABBA'S CHILD

1. Joachim Jeremias, *The Parables of Jesus* (New York: Scribner, 1970), 128.

2. Gerald G. May, M. D., *Addiction and Grace* (San Francisco, CA: HarperCollins, 1988), 168.

3. Richard J. Foster, *Prayer: Finding the Heart's True Home* (San Francisco, CA: HarperOne, 1992), 85.

4. Hans Küng, *On Being a Christian* (New York: Doubleday, 1976), 32.

5. Küng, 33.

6. Donald Gray, *Jesus: The Way to Freedom* (Winona, MN: St. Mary's College Press, 1979), 70.

7. Stephen Covey, *The Seven Habits of Highly Effective People: Powerful Lessons in Personal Change*, Audio Cassette Seminar (Provo, UT: Center for Strategic Leadership, 1984).

8. "Fox Hunt," *Life*, March 13, 1944, 67–69.

9. Alan Jones, *Exploring Spiritual Direction: An Essay in Christian Friendship* (Minneapolis, MN: Winston Press, 1982), 17. This book and another by Jones, *Soul Making: The Desert Way of Spirituality* (Harper & Row, 1985), have been a source of deep insight and endless meditation.

10. Henri J. M. Nouwen, *Life of the Beloved: Spiritual Living in a Secular World* (New York: Crossroad, 1992), 34.

11. Robert J. Wicks, *Touching the Holy: Ordinariness, Self-Esteem, and Friendship* (Notre Dame, IN: Ave Maria Press, 1992), 87. The theme of this little gem of a book is that true ordinariness is tangible holiness. Drawing on the experience of contemporary Christians and the wisdom of the desert fathers and mothers, Wicks says, "The Spirit of ordinariness invites each of us to . . . find out what our inner motivations and talents are and then to express them without reserve or self-consciousness."

12. Adapted from Wendell Berry, *The Hidden Wound* (San Francisco, CA: North Point Press, 1989), 4. I appropriated Berry's thoughts and words on his struggle with racism and expanded them to include homosexuality.

13. Frederich Buechner, *The Clown in the Belfry: Writings on Faith and Fiction* (San Francisco, CA: HarperSanFrancisco, 1992), 146.

14. Anthony De Mello, *The Way to Love: Meditations for Life* (New York: Doubleday, 1991), 77.

CHAPTER FIVE — THE PHARISEE AND THE CHILD

1. Bertrand Russell, *Why I Am Not a Christian: And Other Essays on Religion and Related Subjects* (New York: Simon & Schuster, 1957), 35.

2. Anthony De Mello, *The Way to Love: Meditations for Life* (New York: Doubleday, 1991), 54.

3. Eugene C. Kennedy, *The Choice to Be Human: Jesus Alive in the Gospel of Matthew* (New York: Doubleday, 1985), 211.

4. Kennedy, 128.

5. Thomas Moore, *Care of the Soul: A Guide for Cultivating Depth and Sacredness in Everyday Life* (New York: HarperCollins, 1992), 166.

6. Kennedy, 211.

7. Kennedy, 211.

8. Alan Jones, *Soul Making: The Desert Way of Spirituality* (New York: HarperCollins, 1989), 37.

9. James Finley, *Merton's Palace of Nowhere: A Search for God Through Awareness of the True Self* (Notre Dame, IN: Ave Maria Press, 1978), 54.

10. Simon Tugwell, *The Beatitudes: Soundings in Christian Traditions* (Springfield, IL: Templegate Publishers, 1980), 138. Here I came across the quotation of Thérèse of Lisieux.

11. Brennan Manning, *A Stranger to Self-Hatred: A Glimpse of Jesus* (Denville, NJ: Dimension Books, 1982), 97.

12. Anthony De Mello, *Awareness: A Spirituality Conference in His Own Words* (New York: Doubleday, 1990), 28.

13. John Shea, *Starlight: Beholding the Christmas Miracle All Year Long* (New York: Crossroad, 1993), 92. A seminal thinker who has profoundly touched my life and deepened my understanding of the gospel, Shea's book develops the idea that Christmas is not one day of naïveté and idealism in a year of unrelenting realism. It is the day of the real in a year of illusion. If we wake up on Christmas morning, we may realize we have been sleepwalking through the rest of the year.

14. John L. McKenzie, *The Power and the Wisdom: An Interpretation of the New Testament* (New York: Doubleday, 1972), 208.

15. De Mello, *The Way to Love*, 73.

16. Brennan Manning, *The Gentle Revolutionaries: Breaking Through to Christian Maturity* (Denville, NJ: Dimension Books, 1976), 39.

17. De Mello, *The Way to Love*, 76.

18. William McNamara, *Mystical Passion: Spirituality for a Bored Society* (Amity, NY: Amity House, 1977), 57.

19. Jeffrey D. Imbach, *The Recovery of Love: Christian Mysticism and the Addictive Society* (New York: Crossroad, 1992), 103.

20. Jean Gill, *Unless You Become Like a Little Child: Seeking the Inner Child in Our Spiritual Journey* (New York: Paulist, 1985), 39.

21. Anne Tyler, *Saint Maybe* (New York: Simon & Schuster, 1982), 124.

22. Frederick Buechner, *The Magnificent Defeat* (San Francisco, CA: Harper & Row, 1966), 135.

CHAPTER SIX — PRESENT RISENNESS

1. H. A. Williams, *True Resurrection* (London: Mitchell Begley Limited, 1972), 5.

2. Williams, 5.

3. William A. Barry, *God's Passionate Desire and Our Response* (Notre Dame, IN: Ave Maria Press, 1993), 109.

4. John Shea, *Starlight: Beholding the Christmas Miracle All Year Long* (New York: Crossroad, 1993), 165. The words *Thus, thou shalt not die* are excerpted from Gabriel Marcel's *The Mystery of Being, Volume II: Faith and Reality* (Chicago, IL: Henry Regnery Press, 1960), 171.

5. "A Conversation with Frederick Buechner" *Image: A Journal of the Arts and Religion* (Spring 1989): 56–57.

6. Brennan Manning, *The Ragamuffin Gospel: Good News for the Bedraggled, Beat-Up, and Burnt Out* (Portland, OR: Multnomah, 1990), 89.

7. Edward Schillebeeckx, *For the Sake of the Gospel* (New York: Crossroad, 1992), 73.

8. Schillebeeckx, 73.

9. Peter G. van Breeman, *Certain as the Dawn* (Denville, NJ: Dimension Books, 1980), 83. Here I came across Garaudy's surprising statement.

10. Barry, 87. In a chapter entitled "Mysticism in Hell," Barry relates the astonishing story of the Dutch Jewess who journaled her conviction that God was not absent in the concentration camp.

11. Anne Tyler, *Saint Maybe* (New York: Simon & Schuster, 1982), 199–200.

12. Dom Aelred Watkin, *The Heart of the World* (London: Burns and Dates, 1954), 94.

13. Barry, 115.

14. Harper Lee, *To Kill a Mockingbird* (New York: Grand Central Publishing, 1982), 374.

15. van Breeman, 125. I relied on the Dutch Jesuit with a doctoral degree in atomic physics for the schema of the four main points while developing them in a considerably different manner.

16. Herman Wouk, *Inside, Outside* (New York: Little, Brown, 1985), 185–186.

17. F. M. Cornford, quoted in *Source: What the Bible Says About the Problems of Contemporary Life* by John McKenzie (Chicago: Thomas More Press, 1984), 206.

18. Richard Schickel, "More Than a Heart Warmer: Frank Capra: 1897–1991," *Time* 138, no. 11 (September 16, 1991): 77. Extracted by Walter J. Burghardt, *When Christ Meets Christ: Homilies on the Just Word* (Mahwah, NJ: Paulist, 1993), 77.

19. M. Scott Peck, *The Road Less Traveled* (New York: Touchstone, 2003), 15–16.

CHAPTER SEVEN — THE RECOVERY OF PASSION

1. Thomas Moore, *Care of the Soul: A Guide for Cultivating Depth and Sacredness in Everyday Life* (San Francisco, CA: HarperCollins, 1992), 200.

2. Joachim Jeremias, *The Parables of Jesus* (New York: Scribner, 1970), 84.

3. Associated Press, "Powerball Winner Hiding Out, Planning Charitable Gifts," *Seattle Times*, July 11, 1993.

4. Jeffrey D. Imbach, *The Recovery of Love: Christian Mysticism and the Addictive Society* (New York: Crossroad, 1992), 134.

5. John Shea, *Starlight: Beholding the Christmas Miracle All Year Long* (New York: Crossroad, 1993), 115–117. This story, courtesy of Reuben Gold and the Hasidic tradition, was drastically reworked by Shea. The latter's early works, *Stories of Faith* and *Stories of God*, are a treasure trove of modern parables coupled with a brilliant analysis of the power of storytelling.

6. Beatrice Bruteau, *Radical Optimism: Rooting Ourselves in Reality* (New York: Crossroad, 1993), 99. She is the founder of a school of prayer in Pfafftown, North Carolina, and a trustworthy guide to contemplative consciousness.

7. Robert J. Wicks, *Touching the Holy: Ordinariness, Self-Esteem, and Friendship* (Notre Dame, IN: Ave Maria Press, 1992), 14. Wicks cites these words of Lonergan, which radically affirm that every authentic religious experience is an encounter with infinite Love.

8. "Introduction to Saint John" in *The Jerusalem Bible* (Garden City, NY: Doubleday, 1966), 144.

9. Brennan Manning, *Lion and Lamb: The Relentless Tenderness of Jesus* (Old Tappan, NJ: Revell/Chosen, 1986), 129–130. Now available through Baker (Grand Rapids, MI). Quoting from one's own previously published works is a desperate measure, but sales are slipping and I need a pair of sandals.

10. William Barry, *God's Passionate Desire and Our Response* (Notre Dame, IN: Ave Maria Press, 1993), 33. Quoting from Donne's *Holy Sonnets*, 14.

11. Raymond Brown, *The Churches the Apostles Left Behind* (New York/Ramsey: Paulist, 1984), 93. A very pastoral book with a strong ecumenical flavor that examines the strengths and weaknesses of the various New Testament churches. His careful analysis has luminous insights and vital relevance for contemporary church life.

12. Henri Nouwen, *In the Name of Jesus: Reflections on Christian Leadership* (New York: Crossroad, 1989), 42. An illuminating and inspiring study of leadership in the church based on biblical criteria.

13. Brown, 97.

14. Thomas J. Tyrell, *Urgent Longings: Reflections on the Experience of Infatuation, Human Intimacy, and Contemplative Love* (Whitinsville, MA: Affirmation Books, 1980), 17.

CHAPTER EIGHT — FORTITUDE AND FANTASY

1. Anthony De Mello, *The Way to Love: Meditations for Life* (New York: Doubleday, 1991), 63–64.

2. Peter G. van Breeman, *Called by Name* (Denville, NJ: Dimension Books, 1976), 88.

3. Søren Kierkegaard, quoted by van Breeman, 39.

4. Johannes B. Metz, *Poverty of Spirit* (New York/Mahwah, NJ: Paulist, 1968), 39–40. This fifty-three page spiritual classic, in its umpteenth printing, captures in words of compelling beauty and insight the key message of the gospel: Our great human possibilities are realized only through our radical dependence on God, our poverty of spirit.

5. Johannes B. Metz, *Poverty of Spirit* (Mahwah, NJ: Paulist, 1998), 38.

6. Metz (1968 ed.), 39.

7. Nicholas Harnan, *The Heart's Journey Home* (Notre Dame, IN: Ave Maria Press, 1992), 132–133.

8. Beatrice Bruteau, *Radical Optimism: Rooting Ourselves in Reality* (New York: Crossroad, 1993), 95.

9. Sebastian Moore, *The Fire and the Rose Are One* (New York: Seabury Press, 1980), 14. In three dense and brilliant works, including *Let This Mind Be in You* and *The Crucified Jesus Is No Stranger*, Moore, a monk of Downside Abbey, England, and frequent lecturer in the States, develops the theme of the reconciliation of all things in Christ.

10. Simon Tugwell, *The Beatitudes: Soundings in Christian Tradition* (Springfield, IL: Templegate Publishers, 1980), 54–55.

11. Maurice Blondel, quoted in *Jesus: The Man and the Myth* by James Mackey (New York: Paulist, 1979), 148. Quoted in an earlier work of mine, *A Glimpse of Jesus: The Stranger to Self-Hatred*.

12. Yves Congar, quoted by Avery Dulles in *Models of Revelation* (Garden City, NY: Doubleday, 1983), 161.

13. Eugene Kennedy, *The Choice to Be Human: Jesus Alive in the Gospel of Matthew* (New York: Doubleday, 1985), 117.

14. Edward Schillebeeckx, *For the Sake of the Gospel* (New York: Crossroad, 1992), 28.

15. Walter Burghardt, *Tell the Next Generation: Homilies and Near Homilies* (New York: Paulist, 1980), 315.

16. Iris Murdoch, *The Nice and the Good* (New York: Penguin Books, 1978), 315.

17. William Johnston, *Being in Love: The Practice of Christian Prayer* (San Francisco, CA: Harper & Row, 1989), 99.

CHAPTER NINE — THE RABBI'S HEARTBEAT

1. Eugene Peterson, *Reversed Thunder: The Revelation of John and the Praying Imagination* (New York: Harper & Row, 1989), 17.

2. John Shea, *An Experience Named Spirit* (Chicago, IL: Thomas More Press, 1986), 166. Here I have appropriated Shea's words about the rejected heart and applied them to the cynical heart, believing they are essentially the same.

3. H. H. Price, *Belief* (London: Allen and Unwin, 1969), 40. Quoted in H. A. Williams's *True Resurrection* (London: Mitchell Begley Limited, 1972).

4. Viktor Frankl, *Psychotherapy and Existentialism: Selected Papers on Logotherapy* (New York: Simon & Schuster, 1967), 9.

5. Eugene Kennedy, *The Choice to Be Human: Jesus Alive in the Gospel of Matthew* (New York: Doubleday, 1985), 14.

6. Sebastian Moore, *The Crucified Jesus Is No Stranger* (Mahwah, NJ: Paulist, 1977), 35.

7. Sebastian Moore, 37.

8. Sebastian Moore, 37.

9. John Cobb, *The Structure of Christian Existence* (Philadelphia, PA: Westminster, 1968), 135. Quoted by Shea, 220.

10. H. A. Williams, *True Resurrection* (London: Mitchell Begley Limited, 1972), 157.

11. James K. Baxter, *Jerusalem Daybook* (Wellington, New Zealand: Price, Milburn and Co., 1971), 2. I rewrote the story in certain places. None of the changes altered the meaning of the story.

12. Thomas Moore, *Care of the Soul: A Guide for Cultivating Depth and Sacredness in Everyday Life* (San Francisco, CA: HarperCollins, 1992), 263.

13. Thomas Moore, 112.

14. Sebastian Moore, 99.

15. Sebastian Moore, 100.

16. Schalom Ben-Chorin, quoted by Hans Küng in *The Church* (New York: Sheed and Ward, 1968), 149.

17. I enthusiastically recommend three books that offer helpful and practical recommendations for developing and sustaining the awareness of present risenness: The time-honored classic by Brother Lawrence—*The Practice of the Presence of God*—and two more recent works—*The Awakened Heart: Opening Yourself to the Love You Need* by Gerald G. May (HarperOne) and *Radical Optimism: Rooting Ourselves in Reality* by Beatrice Bruteau (Crossroad).

18. Donald Gray, *Jesus: the Way to Freedom* (Winona, MN: St. Mary's Press, 1979), 69.

19. Jürgen Moltmann, *The Trinity and the Kingdom: The Doctrine of God* (Minneapolis, MN: Augsburg, 1993), 23. Quoted by Alan Jones in *Soul Making: The Desert Way of Spirituality* (Harper & Row, 1985).

INTERNALIZING THE BOOK: GUIDE FOR GROUP STUDY

1. Eugene Kennedy, *The Choice to Be Human: Jesus Alive in the Gospel of Matthew* (New York: Doubleday, 1985), 14.

About the Author

In the springtime of Depression-era New York City, BRENNAN MANNING—christened Richard Francis Xavier—was born to Emmett and Amy Manning. He grew up in Brooklyn along with his brother, Robert, and sister, Geraldine. After graduating from high school and attending St. John's University (Queens, New York) for two years, he enlisted in the U.S. Marine Corps and was sent overseas to fight in the Korean War.

Upon his return, Brennan began a program in journalism at the University of Missouri. But he departed after a semester, restlessly searching for something "more" in life. "Maybe the something 'more' is God," an advisor had suggested, triggering Brennan's enrollment in a Catholic seminary in Loretto, Pennsylvania.

In February 1956, while Brennan was meditating on the Stations of the Cross, a powerful experience of the personal love of Jesus Christ sealed the call of God on his life. "At that moment," he later recalled, "the entire Christian life became for me an intimate, heartfelt relationship with Jesus." Four years later, he graduated from St. Francis College (major in philosophy; minor in Latin) and went on to complete four years of advanced studies in theology. May 1963 marked his graduation from St. Francis Seminary and ordination to the Franciscan priesthood.

Brennan's ministry responsibilities in succeeding years took him from the hallways of academia to the byways of the poor: theology instructor and campus minister at the University of Steubenville; liturgy instructor and spiritual director at St. Francis Seminary; graduate student in creative writing at Columbia University, and in Scripture and liturgy at Catholic University of America; and living and working among the poor in Europe and the U.S.

A two-year leave of absence from the Franciscans took Brennan to Spain in the late sixties. He joined the Little Brothers of Jesus of Charles de Foucauld, an Order committed to an uncloistered, contemplative life among the poor—a lifestyle of days spent in manual labor and nights wrapped in silence and prayer. Among his many and varied assignments, Brennan became an *aguador* (water carrier), transporting water to rural villages via donkey and buckboard; a mason's assistant, shoveling mud and straw in the blazing Spanish heat; a dishwasher in France; a voluntary prisoner in a Swiss jail, his identity as a priest known only to the warden; and a solitary contemplative secluded in a remote cave for six months in the Zaragoza desert.

During his retreat in the isolated cave, Brennan was once again powerfully convicted by the revelation of God's love in the crucified Christ. On a midwinter's night, he received this word from the Lord: "For love of you I left my Father's side. I came to you who ran from me, who fled me, who did not want to hear my name. For love of you I was covered with spit, punched and beaten, and fixed to the wood of the cross." Brennan would later reflect, "Those words are burned into my life. That night, I learned what a wise old Franciscan told me the day I joined the Order—'Once you come to know the love of Jesus Christ, nothing else in the world will seem as beautiful or desirable.'"

The early seventies found Brennan back in the U.S. as he and four other priests established an experimental community in the bustling seaport city of Bayou La Batre, Alabama. Seeking to model the primitive life of the Franciscans, the fathers settled in a house on Mississippi Bay and quietly went to work on shrimp boats, ministering to the shrimpers and their families who had drifted out of reach from the church. Next to the community house was a chapel that had been destroyed by

Hurricane Camille. The fathers restored it and offered a Friday night liturgy and social event, which soon became a popular gathering and precipitated many families' return to engagement in the local church.

From Alabama, Brennan moved to Ft. Lauderdale, Florida, in the mid-1970s and resumed campus ministry at Broward Community College. His successful ministry was harshly interrupted, however, when he suffered a precipitate collapse into alcoholism. Six months of treatment, culminating at the Hazelden treatment center in Minnesota, restored his health and placed him on the road to recovery.

It was at this point in his life that Brennan began writing in earnest. One book soon followed upon another as invitations for him to speak and to lead spiritual retreats multiplied exponentially. The new and renewed directions in which God's call was taking Brennan eventually led him out of the Franciscan Order. In 1982, he married Roslyn Ann Walker and settled in New Orleans.

Brennan was a popular speaker and bestselling author. He traveled widely, writing and preaching, to encourage men and women everywhere to accept and embrace the good news of God's unconditional love in Jesus Christ. Brennan went home to be with his Abba on April 12, 2013.

Other Books by Brennan Manning:

Prophets and Lovers (Dimension Books, 1976)

The Gentle Revolutionaries (Dimension Books, 1976)

The Wisdom of Accepted Tenderness (Dimension Books, 1978)

Souvenirs of Solitude (Dimension Books, 1979)

A Stranger to Self-Hatred (Dimension Books, 1982)

Lion and Lamb (Revell/Chosen, 1986)

The Ragamuffin Gospel (Multnomah, 1990)

The Signature of Jesus (Multnomah, 1996)

The Boy Who Cried Abba: A Parable of Trust and Acceptance
(Multnomah,1996)

*Reflections for Ragamuffins: Daily Devotions from the Writings of
Brennan Manning* (HarperOne,1998)

Ruthless Trust: The Ragamuffin's Path to God (HarperOne, 2001)

*The Wisdom of Tenderness: What Happens When God's Fierce Mercy
Transforms Our Lives* (HarperOne, 2002)

The Journey of the Prodigal: A Parable of Sin and Redemption
(Crossroad, 2002)

A Glimpse of Jesus: The Stranger to Self-Hatred
(HarperSanFrancisco, 2003)

The Importance of Being Foolish: How to Think like Jesus
(HarperOne, 2006)

The Furious Longing of God (Cook Communications, 2009)

Souvenirs of Solitude: Finding Rest in Abba's Embrace
(NavPress, 2009)

Patched Together: A Story of My Story (Cook Communications, 2010)

All Is Grace: A Ragamuffin Memoir (Cook Communications, 2011)

To order books and CDs by Brennan Manning, contact Willie Juan
Ministries, PO Box 6911, New Orleans, LA 70114; 504-393-2567.

About the 2015 Edition Editor

JOHN BLASE preached for over a decade; but then he thought he'd go
where the money is, so he started writing poetry. He's a lucky man with a
stunning wife and three kids who look like their mother. They all live in
Colorado. His books include *Know When to Hold 'Em: The High Stakes
Game of Fatherhood*; *Touching Wonder: Recapturing the Awe of Christmas*;
and *All Is Grace: A Ragamuffin Memoir* (cowritten with Brennan Manning).
He ponders faithfully at www.thebeautifuldue.wordpress.com.

About the Cover Illustrator

CHARLIE MACKESY is English. He slowly came to faith in Jesus from atheism and still struggles with institutionalized religion. He feels that humans function best in the context of love and is excited by the notion that that is who God is. Painting has been his way of praying, and he loves to make work that helps people sink into the peaceful understanding that they are known, loved, forgiven, and free. This painting was made for a friend who always struggled to believe that God could love him.

THERE'S GOOD NEWS FOR THE WEARY.

BILL TELL

lay it down

LIVING IN THE FREEDOM
OF THE GOSPEL

Bill Tell | 978-1-61291-820-4

Be set free by the overwhelming grace of God.

Available at NavPress.com or wherever
Christian books are sold.

CP0889

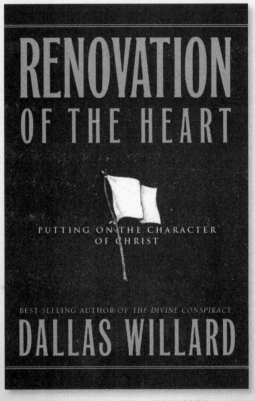